Susan C. Vaughan, M.D.

HALF EMPTY
HALF FULL

*Understanding the
Psychological Roots
of Optimism*

HARCOURT, INC.
New York   San Diego   London

Library of Congress Cataloging-in-Publication Data
Vaughan, Susan C.
Half empty, half full: understanding the psychological roots of
optimism/Susan C. Vaughan.
p.   cm.
Includes bibliographical references and index.
ISBN 0-15-100401-3
1. Optimism.   I. Title.
BF698.35.O57 V38 2000
152.4—dc21   99-058575

Designed by Linda Lockowitz
Text set in Adobe Garamond
Printed in the United States of America
First edition
A C E G I K J'H F D B

For my analyst, Robert Alan Glick, M.D.,
with deep appreciation for all that he has given
me, my family, and my patients

Contents

Acknowledgments

THANKS TO MY PATIENTS, past and present. Although none will find themselves in the pages of this book, the fictional "patients" I discuss herein are drawn from their experiences. In allowing me to understand with them how their minds work, they have given me the privilege and opportunity to garner the insights about mood modulation that led to this book. I hope that in return I have helped them live happier, fuller lives, and that some of the things we learned together might in turn help the readers of this book.

The Department of Psychiatry at the Columbia University College of Physicians and Surgeons and the Columbia Center for Psychoanalytic Training and Research in particular have been my intellectual home these past fifteen years, and I appreciate all that my friends and colleagues have taught me over the years as well as the collegial atmosphere that allowed me to research and think through the issues in this book. Special thanks to Steven Roose, Stanley Bone,

Elizabeth Auchicloss, Roger MacKinnon, and Myron Hofer.

My fabulous editor Jane Isay encouraged me throughout the ups and downs of writing this book, giving me the space and time yet support I needed to finally say what I was trying to say about optimism. Thanks to Leigh Weiner for shepherding the book through the production process. Thanks to the team at Harcourt for believing in this book and, more generally, for believing in the intelligence and sophistication of readers. My agent, Joy Harris, has encouraged my growth as a writer but also helped me focus my sometimes scattered interests in a productive manner. Thanks also to her assistants Kassandra Duane and Leslie Daniels for their support and for handling the logistical hassles along the way. Many thanks to my former editors at *Harper's Bazaar,* especially Susan Kittenplan and Annemarie Iverson for their ongoing interest in this project as well as for giving me the assignments that provided much needed breaks along the way. Thanks also to my electronic friend Bob Duffy for his thoughtful running commentary on the process of writing this book and his certainty that I had something of interest to say on the subject.

Deb Wasser's love and support provide the nourishment in which this book and every other important project in my life takes root; our relationship has given me the room to grow personally and professionally. In addition, her intelligence and willingness to converse, debate, and critique helped to clarify and improve my ideas.

Finally, my deepest gratitude to my analyst, Robert Alan Glick, M.D., and to my daughter, Savannah Wynn. Through my relationships with both I have come to understand in a deeply personal way the subject of this book.

Preface

IN MAURICE SENDAK'S perennially popular children's book *Where the Wild Things Are,* Max, in his wolf suit, makes mischief of one kind and another until his mother, in exasperation, calls him a wild thing. "I'll eat you up!" Max says menacingly, and is sent to bed without his supper. In his dreams he travels to "the place where the wild things are," and they "roar their terrible roars and gnash their terrible teeth and roll their terrible eyes and show their terrible claws" until Max commands "Be still!" and tames them with the magic trick of staring into all their yellow eyes without blinking.

This book is about the wild things within each of us, the tumult of inner feelings that each of us must learn to tame. As Max's experience suggests, our emotions can get us into trouble in relationships. But they are also essential if we are to conjure the creatures that make life interesting. Ultimately, it is our ability to learn to control our feelings without quashing them that gives us the capacity for an optimistic view of ourselves and the world around us. Optimism depends upon our ability to become the king of all the wild things. As we shall see in this book, it requires mothers or others who will send us to bed without supper but who will keep it warm as well, ready for us when we return, lonely, from where the wild things are. Optimism arises from the inner controls that these early life experiences give us, controls that are etched in the circuitry of our brains. But as we'll see, if you're still struggling with inner monsters in adulthood and the pessimistic perspective on yourself and the world that they bring, there is hope. Because optimism and pessimism are the result of our inner process of mood regulation, and like other processes, we can improve it with practice, learn the magic tricks we need to make us king. Let the wild rumpus begin!

HALF EMPTY
HALF FULL

Chapter One

THE ILLUSION
OF AN ISLAND

ONCE UPON A TIME a scientist broke the rats in his laboratory into random groups. The rats in the first group were placed one by one in a big tank of water made opaque with milk. They had to swim for a set amount of time. These rats were the lucky ones, since their tank had a tiny island hidden under the water on which they could perch without having to swim. Their island was always in a fixed location in the tank, there for them to find without fail, a way of getting a tiny leg up and a respite from the swim.

The rats in the second group swam for exactly the same amount of time in the milky water as those in the first group. But their tank had no island, no oasis amid the vast vat. After their swims, the rats in both groups were plucked from the water, weary and be-draggled. Both groups then rested, ate, and otherwise recuperated before the real Rat Race.

When the big day came, both groups of rats were at it again. The researcher once again made them swim one by one. But this time all the rats swam in a tank without an island. Much as they swam, there was simply no oasis to be found, no respite from having to paddle like mad just to stay afloat. The researcher rescued them before their whiskered noses slipped beneath the water. Then he carefully recorded precisely where and for how long each rat swam before returning it to its cage, wet and waterlogged, probably surprised to be alive.

When the scientist tallied up the time each rat spent in the tank, imagine how surprised he was. He found that those lucky rodent racers whose island had been there for them the first time swam for over twice as long, looking for the island where it had previously been. In contrast, those who had never found a predictable foothold in their hour of need were reduced to wandering aimlessly around the tank, swimming in seemingly directionless circles, chasing their tails in vain as they looked for a means of escape.[1]

Now, you may find it a stretch to say that the rats that had experienced a consistent island in their prior swims were optimistic. But given that they were broken randomly into two groups in the first place, how else can we understand what kept them looking for twice as long as their competitors rather than paddling haphazardly around the tank? Isn't their belief that there is something definite to swim for a positive expectation rooted in the reality of their earlier experience? Since there was no island in the tank in which they took their second swim, isn't it fair to say that what made the difference as to whether they sank or swam was the illusion of an island, their ability to conjure an inner image of an island to swim for when the going got rough, even if such an island existed only in their imagination?

In this book I will argue that optimism depends upon our ability to construct and sustain the illusion of an island. I will show why I think this ability is the result of a series of inner psychological processes that can be improved upon with practice, a set of psychological maneuvers through which we shift our perspective, refocus our vision. But if you hold a traditional view of optimism and pessimism, you probably believe that optimism depends instead on whether you see the proverbial glass as half empty or half full. And if you tend to see the glass as half empty then chances are you think that's just the way you are and there's nothing you can do about it anyway. After all, people are optimists or pessimists by nature, aren't they? It's a trait, a matter of inborn temperament, a fixed and immutable fact of biology, isn't it? While we've long recognized that optimism pervades and influences almost everything—our thoughts, our feelings, our perspective in life, even our ability to keep on swimming in the face of adversity—we've also long believed that asking a pessimistic person to be more optimistic is like asking a leopard to change his spots.

If this is how you've thought about optimism until now, you're in good company. After all, even the *Oxford English Dictionary* defines optimism as a "disposition to hope for the best or to look on the bright side of things; a general tendency to take a favorable view of circumstances or prospects." Contained in the words *disposition* and *general tendency* is the implication that optimism is a stable aspect of character. If we were to accept this definition—and we have—we would believe that Eeyore is about as likely to look on the bright side as Tigger is to lose the spring in his step.

Yet I believe we would be wrong, and that in our error we might add our tendency to see the glass as either half empty or half full to the long and growing list of biological imperatives—like height or eye color or an ovarian cancer gene—that we simply have to live with, matters of genetic destiny. If optimism were really an inborn trait, you wouldn't be able to change it much.

But if I thought that optimism were biological alone, a trait of personality, then it would be cruel to write this book, the equivalent of showing Moses the Promised Land but never allowing him to enter. I believe that optimism is the result of an internal process of illusion building. In this book I will show why we should fundamentally redefine optimism as the result of a particular series of mental machinations, psychological somersaults. These internal gymnastics are not generally something that optimists are just born knowing how to do. Optimism is not, to paraphrase Emily Dickinson on hope, "a thing with feathers that perches in the breast." Instead it is an active internal process, more akin to learning to fly. It is a verb, not a noun. And pessimism, by contrast, is not the absence of some elusive winged creature that our biological birdcage either contains or lacks. That's good news, because if optimism is the result of inner psychological processes, then we can all become better illusion-builders with practice. So if you can't imagine that illusive island now, don't worry. You can learn to.

Why would we want to learn to sustain such a fiction anyway, searching for an illusory island that may not be there at all? After all, an illusion is defined as "a false impression or belief, a delusion, an incorrect perception"—not something that a psychiatrist and psychoanalyst such as myself would normally advocate cultivating as a regular habit, a way of living life. Aren't illusions the stuff of magic acts? Entertaining at best, but fundamentally a distraction from real life? Although illusions may enchant us, don't they keep us from looking reality square in the eye and doing the things we need to do to change our real-life situations? After all, if we sat in the movies day after day, we might enjoy some amazing illusions, but they wouldn't alter the reality we faced when we left the theater, blinking in the glare of our problems. Wouldn't illusions seduce us into living in a fantasy world at the expense of the real one? Shouldn't we get just get real instead? Doesn't our psychological health depend upon it?

In fact, studies suggest that reality is overrated. People who are the most closely in touch with reality are probably depressed. For example, in one study, depressed people were much more accurate than those who were not currently depressed at estimating the risks of all sorts of disasters befalling them, from plane crashes to their chances of being hit and killed by a bus when crossing the street on any given day. They saw the dangers of life head-on and estimated them accurately. Psychologists call it "depressive realism." In contrast, nondepressed people are off the mark when asked about the odds of various kinds of negative events—in an optimistic but unrealistic, inaccurate way.[2] When we look at reality stripped bare of the illusions I consider crucial, what we are really seeing is our fundamental helplessness and lack of control in the face of an indifferent universe, our elemental aloneness, our failure to achieve successes that can change the basic parameters of our mortality. And perhaps most importantly, depression and the bald-faced look at reality it provides for us tend to yank us out of our engagement with life, our ability to exist in the moment. Seeing the world this way can even precipitate an existential crisis in which we're left living in a universe in which none of our actions ultimately matter, in which we're just going through the motions waiting for it all to end. As psychiatrist Viktor Frankl concluded after surviving the dismal reality of Auschwitz, we must each search for and ultimately construct our own meanings in order to survive. Looking at reality stripped of all our illusions means being psychically naked, unprotected, and open to despair, depression, even suicide.[3] So despite the emphasis that psychologists and psychiatrists have placed on the importance of "reality testing," it may be that the illusions involved in optimism are actually more psychologically healthy.

In contrast to overrated reality, it is difficult to overemphasize the importance and positive effects of optimism. As you might conclude from the Rat Race, perhaps paramount among the advantages of optimism is that optimists persevere, with continued—and even more determined—activity rather than inertia in the face of adversity. Optimism is also to some extent a self-fulfilling prophecy in the sense that if you look for that island for over twice as long, you better your chances of finding it if it's there. Other people notice and respond positively to the outlook of optimists, giving them an advantage in work, love, and play. In addition to perseverance, optimism breeds popularity and the success that so often accompanies it. Optimistic thinking predicts who will be a successful life insurance salesman as well as which basketball teams will beat their projected point spreads in any given season. A candidate with an optimistic stance has a greater chance of being elected president. And optimistic swimmers who are told their times in an important race are worse than they actually are will do even better the second time around.[4]

When it comes to health and optimism, the jury is in. Even rats who are made helpless respond differently to an injection of potentially lethal tumor cells. When injected with a number of tumor cells from which 50% of a control group live and 50% die, only 27% of helpless, pessimistic rats survive, while 70% of rats who have a more optimistic stance remain alive.[5] Pessimism is just as bad for human health as it is for rat health. It makes people more liable to die of heart disease once they have it as well as more likely to get cancer in the first place. In a study of male Harvard undergraduates from the 1940s, high amounts of optimism at age twenty predicted good health at sixty-five. Meanwhile, those who were highly pessimistic at twenty often had left no forwarding address by the time those questionnaires rolled around at age sixty-five.[6]

Perhaps the main reason being optimistic is worthwhile is that it simply feels better. No matter how long you live or what you do with yourself while you're around, you'll enjoy life more if you can sustain the illusion of an island up ahead, something to swim toward. You'll spend more time feeling engaged, hopeful, and happy and less time feeling depressed, anxious, or angry. Given the choice of viewing life through the rose-colored glasses of hope rather than the dark blinders of sadness, anger, and worry, wouldn't it be far better to assume you'll find a foothold amid the chaos? After all, even if you go under, won't you have enjoyed the swim all the more if you sustain hope until the end rather than sinking into despair? Although optimism is the result of an illusion, it is a desirable distortion of reality.

But what exactly does this illusion do for us? And how does it lead to optimism? I'll argue that the island's importance is that it gives us something to swim toward when we feel overwhelmed, tired to the bone, and in danger of giving up and going under. By giving us such a goal, the illusory islands that optimists construct help them fend off negative feelings and keep them feeling autonomous and centered, the skippers of their own ships. Like a beacon on the horizon to aim for when sailing on a stormy sea, the illusion of an island allows us to look beyond the menacing problems (and the waves of emotions they produce) that we're currently battling toward a future in which we will be standing securely on dry land once more. In this case the beacon cannot be purely external in order to work well over the course of a lifetime. It must be present within us, and we must be able to cast its internal light onto the horizon so that we can see it when we most need it. Through my own research and years of experience in clinical practice, I've come to believe that the real reason to sustain the illusion of an island on the horizon is that it gives us hope amid stormy seas.

In the upcoming chapters, I'll show how I arrived at the conclusion that optimism is the illusion of an island. First, in chapter 2, I'll discuss the fact that though we're wont to focus only on the external monsters of life, it's actually the projection of our own "beasts within" that is the real threat to optimism. The most resilient optimists are those who realize they can defy all external foes, regardless of what their day dishes out, by mastering themselves, their inner emotions, and their perspective on life. The fundamental good news embedded in my new view of optimism is that, because becoming optimistic is an active process, we can all achieve greater mastery with practice. In chapter 3, I'll explore the fundamental link between our ability to soothe the sometimes seething cauldron of feelings within ourselves and our ability to sustain the illusion of controlling the world around us. In chapter 4, I'll show you the biological roots of optimism and what we're trying to do, in neurobiological terms, when we shift our perspective toward a more optimistic stance. It's in this chapter that we'll also see how the brain circuitry develops in the crucible of early life experiences. Chapter 5 goes on to argue that it's the problematic lessons of childhood that become the breeding ground of pessimism, leaving us to struggle long into adult life with negative views of our self and our place in the world. In chapter 6, patient studies will illustrate that when we can't regulate how we feel we become overly dependent on others, demanding their emotional reactions to bolster our flagging sense of self. Then chapter 7 will teach several specific ways to improve your current level of optimism. (Here's the how-tos. Feel free to peek ahead.) My techniques center on certain ways to shift your thinking, refocus your vision, and assume a positive perspective. We'll take a look at some unusual experiments that prove: if you can't feel it, fake it. Tricking the limbic system via physical effects can make illusions a real self-fulfilling prophecy. In chapter 8, we'll watch a master illusionist in action, an extraordinarily brave man who builds islands despite the most daunting of odds. Finally, in chapter 9, I'll tell you how my view of optimism fits into an exciting new intellectual movement know as positive psychology. By taking a new look at what makes us happy instead of focusing on anxiety, aggression, and depression as traditional psychology has done, I believe we're poised to learn more about how to achieve the optimistic path.

Over the course of this book, you'll see how much optimism depends on our ability to construct and sustain that beacon of strength inside—an illusion of an island to swim to when the going gets rough. I'll show to a much more substantial degree than you probably think right now that optimists are made, not born. But the real trick is that, as we learn the skills we need to sustain the illusion of an island on the horizon, we're actually building a real internal psychological core of strength. Our practice at illusion-building ultimately gives rise to an authentic inner island. And as this psychological ground coalesces underfoot, we find we have a place inside ourselves to stand on that gives us a genuine leg up on the rat race we all face in daily life.

Chapter Two

GORILLAS IN OUR MIDST

I dreamed that I was at the zoo with my mother when the gorillas broke out of their cages. Everyone around us was running and shouting and I felt scared to death. My mother and I hid in the giraffe house but it seemed that the gorillas were closing in. When I looked down at my coat it was changing back and forth from fabric to fur, fabric to fur, fabric to fur. I felt panicky and anxious.

WHEN WE REFLECT upon what affects our ability to feel optimistic, somehow we usually seem to focus on the gorillas outside, those external monsters beyond our control that threaten to unexpectedly escape their cages and pursue us while we are innocently enjoying the zoo, just minding our own business. We're sure it's the real monsters who lurk just around the next corner that are raising our anxiety level, making us pessimistic. But as my patient Vicky's dream hints, the gorillas are not merely out there, testing the bars of their cages as they prepare to threaten our peace of mind. They are also within us. As she runs to hide in the giraffe house with her mother, attempting to escape the gorillas that seem to be closing in on her, Vicky finds *herself* shifting between girl and gorilla as her coat changes back and forth from fabric to fur. In this chapter I'll show you why I've come to believe that it's actually the beasts within—inner emotions such as anxiety, anger, and sadness that sometimes threaten to overwhelm us—that are the true threats to our capacity for optimism. The real source of our pessimism is not our fear that the world around us is hairy, but rather the much bigger danger that our own beastly feelings are beyond our ability to control.

While we're well aware that spotting a gorilla on the horizon up ahead can make our anxiety level soar, we generally underestimate the reverse: the profound effect that anxiety, anger, and sadness have on our perception of the world around us. Yet in reality the way we experience the external world, including whether or not we expect to encounter King Kong on our next trip to the supermarket, can only be a reflection of our inner feelings. That's because our emotions and the thoughts that accompany them are the lenses through which we process our perspective on the people, places, and events around us. But because that lens so convincingly colors the world around us and because it's an integral part of our minds and brains, we tend to forget that this lens between ourselves and the world outside is even there. We tend to believe instead that we are seeing things "as they are," in the process ignoring the fact that there is no "real" reality, just the one that our minds construct by percolating the experiences we have through the lens of our mood of the moment. So when we look to the world around us to justify an optimistic or pessimistic stance, we forget that the way the world looks—including whether it seems warm and welcoming or dark and foreboding—is actually highly dependent on and shaped by our current internal state. Put simply, a cauldron of complex inner feelings colors what we see and how we see it from moment to moment. When it comes to optimism, it's the rumblings of these inner beasts that matter most.

Like our perspective on the present, our current inner emotional state colors our sense of our past history and our future prospects as well. Our view of the past and future are, similarly, constructions within our own minds that can shift from moment to moment depending on our state of mind. In fact, we can only see the past and the future through the filter of our inner present, making the remembered past and the fantasied future the result of our own constructions based upon where we are right now. If gorillas abound inside us now, threatening our peace of mind and making us anxious, then we cannot help but look for evidence of those primate pursuers all around, as well as expecting to encounter them down the road. Only once we have found a way to soothe the savage feelings within, to return ourselves to an interested, excited, or happy state, can the world around us, our perspectives on the past, and our forecasts for the future contain blue skies once again. I believe we consistently underestimate how much our current inner climate influences whether we appear optimistic or pessimistic as we go about our lives from day to day. In fact, it may be that there is really no such thing as optimism or pessimism independent of our current mood.

As a psychiatrist, I began to appreciate how much optimism is a process rather than a stable state when I watched a bipolar (manic-depressive) patient with extreme highs and lows cycle rapidly. In a manic state, she was sure that her future was bright, certain that she could become a world-famous novelist. But when she was depressed just a few days later she felt certain that suicide was the best course of action. I watched her perspective shift not once, but over and over again according to where she was in her continuing series of ups and downs. I saw that my patient's view of herself and the world around her as well as her expectations about her own future were indeed inseparable from her current inner state.

But what about the rest of us who don't suffer from bipolar cycling? The recent widespread use of antidepressants has demonstrated how, in a large segment of the general population, pessimism can shift instantly and dramatically into optimism. Giving a medication like Prozac to a dysphoric, dysthymic Eeyore can allow him to see the glass half full for the first time ever. As a psychiatrist, watching a patient who believed his pessimistic perspective was simply the way things were change the way he sees himself and all of life is extraordinary.

Of course, thus far my assertions about the crucial relationship between optimism and our mood of the moment are based on anecdotal observations. But I'm not going to ask you to take my word for it. It is clear from several decades of research that how we see ourselves, the world around us, and the prospects for the future at a given moment is very much a product of our current emotional state. It all started with a series of simple studies in which psychologist Gordon Bower asked subjects to recall childhood incidents, then to characterize them as pleasant, unpleasant, or neutral. The next day a happy or sad mood was induced in each subject, and they were asked to recall the incidents they had described the day before. Subjects whose moods were happy had a much greater tendency to recall happy childhood stories, while those who were sad were more likely to recall sad childhood events. Bower also demonstrated that people's moods determined their perspective on what was happening in ambiguous drawings, and that mood influenced which character they would identify with—and recall details about—in a story that contained both a happy and a sad character who met to play a friendly game of tennis.[1] Thus, our emotions also affect our perspectives on others in the world around us, not just our view of ourselves.

Bower's work issued in a flurry of activity among psychologists and psychiatrists interested in this phenomenon, which is known as mood congruence. Mood-congruent effects have an impact on our memory and recall, our perception of events, our in-

terpretations of the world around us, and our perspectives on ourselves and our histories and futures.
Induce a sad mood in nondepressed people by telling
them a sad story, then try to teach them happy and
sad words, and they will absorb the sad words much
more effectively than the happy ones. Make people
moderately more happy with a humorous audiotape,
and more cheerful memories of their childhoods will
emerge. Take the same group the very next day and
make them anxious instead, and the stories they tell
about their past, present, and future will be tinged
with anxious concerns. Make people angry and
they'll see people around them as more hostile, too,
as deliberately trying to get in their way. Take anxious
subjects and ask them to rate whether faces around
them are displaying negative emotions, and watch
their moods bounce right back at them, seemingly
reflected in the anxious and unhappy faces they see in
the world all around them. And ask people when
you've induced in them a sad or anxious mood to
imagine the risks of bad things befalling them down
the road, and watch their once-bright futures turn
dismal before your eyes.[2] But these effects are not
limited to the laboratory. In one recent study of
rapidly cycling bipolar patients asked to recall autobiographical events, their mood of the moment made

all the difference in whether the events that the patients remembered were happy or sad.[3] Another study of over seven hundred (nonpatient) college undergraduates demonstrated that every time they retrieved a memory, especially an autobiographical one or one associated with a word or idea, their memories and associations were affected by their momentary emotional state.[4] To a much larger extent than we generally appreciate, the memories we recall from the past, what we take note of and remember in the present, and what we anticipate about the future are all guided by our current state of mind.

Mood-congruent effects demonstrate just how labile optimism and pessimism really are. Just as a line is composed of individual points, our emotional lives are composed of a series of fluctuating inner states that often shift on a moment-to-moment basis. Down in the mouth Eeyores often get stuck in negative emotions for long periods of time and therefore are caught in the grip of the pessimistic ruminations that these moods produce. In contrast, vibrant Tiggers—who often seem like balls on the ends of strings as they bounce their way through life—are really people who are able to string together moment after moment of well-being in a way that makes it seem effortless, like a baseball team on a winning streak.

Our capacity for optimism also depends upon trusting that we can experience a range of emotions without getting stuck. Optimists allow themselves to feel sad when they see suffering around them, but can still conceive of finding happiness around the next bend. Pessimists often find themselves worrying in advance about when the next big plunge will come, sometimes even helping to precipitate it by constantly listening for evidence that they're nearing the top of their good mood and heading for a nose dive.

It turns out that although many people divide the world into optimists and pessimists in strictly black and white terms, when they're made to analyze themselves in a way they might never have before, everything becomes far more complex.

"I'm a pessimist," my colleague Joseph replied in response to the half-empty, half-full question. "I'm always looking out for the worst, imagining what can go wrong in a situation." He hesitated and gave me a quizzical look. "But that doesn't necessarily mean I think it'll turn out badly. In fact, I guess I feel that I'll be able to see catastrophes before they happen and avert them. It means I spend a lot of time worrying, but in the end I expect things to go well. So maybe that makes me an optimist?"

My friend Stacy admitted that she sometimes secretly worries about becoming a bag lady despite the fact that she was a successful lawyer. "I'm generally an optimist, but there are times when I imagine getting sued and losing everything, even if I've really done nothing wrong. Once I start thinking that way I get anxious, depressed, alarmed, and it's hard for me to get out of it. Or maybe I'm anxious, depressed, and alarmed in the first place, and that's what triggers the dire thoughts. I don't know. Meanwhile, everyone around me sees me as an upbeat, optimistic, can-do kind of person. And in a sense, as long as I'm feeling good, I am. But maybe I'm more of a pessimist than I seem, since I can so easily imagine myself losing everything and winding up homeless and alone. I think the bottom line is that I spend a lot of time forcing myself to act cheerful in hopes of keeping my mood up and fending off anxiety. But underneath the happiness is a sense that I could crash at any moment. It's like living in a minefield."

My patient Vicky, whose dream began this chapter, began to discuss the question of optimism spontaneously in a psychotherapy session, gradually recognizing that she often began to feel pessimistic when things were going a little too well. "I only start to have the sense that there's a gorilla around the next corner when things are going a little too well for me. Like after I was promoted at work, I started to worry about one sentence in a memo I had sent out, and I couldn't stop. It really brought me down. At the time, it seemed like the sentence that would make my bosses realize they'd made a mistake. I would be revealed to be lacking. But in another way, it seemed like I was almost *trying* to take the wind out of my sails, keeping myself from feeling too excited and successful. And it worked, too. I only become really pessimistic when I have lots of objective reasons to be optimistic. When there's less to be excited about, I'm fairly positive about myself and my future." She chuckled at the ironic contradiction inherent in what she was saying.

As these vignettes suggest, optimism arises as the result of an internal sense of control over our own inner states, a kind of self-reliant sense that we can depend on our ability to regulate our inner states. In contrast, pessimism arises when we are less certain of our ability to modulate our moods effectively, when our emotional climate-control mechanisms feel undependable. Joseph finds himself in an anxious mood in response to a perceived threat on the horizon and begins to worry about everything that could go wrong. Through this internal process, he mentally locates, attacks, and solves the problems that he envisions lurking on the horizon. This process proves a productive way to modulate his own inner state as he begins to feel that he will get whatever is coming at him before it gets him. Thus, the process of mulling over the dark possibilities actually reduces his anxiety level, making him feel more internally competent and comfortable, more in control of the inner machinations of his mind. Perhaps there are ultimately better ways to modulate an anxious mood than by slaying each and every imaginable dragon, but his current mood-modulation mechanism does indeed work. Although the churnings of his inner mechanisms may look pessimistic in tone, the *result* of these churnings is a fundamentally optimistic stance toward the future, a sense that he can handle whatever life dishes out. He can depend on himself to alter the climate of his inner world in a positive way.

In contrast, although Stacy may look like more of an optimist on the face of it, she finds she cannot control her cascade of negative thoughts and feelings about being sued and losing everything, once they have started. Her process of worrying leads to psychological entropy, increasing her sense of inner dysregulation and disorder. She begins to experience the world around her as chaotic and dangerous. In her case, worrying produces increasing discomfort, rather than reducing anxiety levels as do my colleague's ruminations. Worrying moves her in the wrong direction, making her feel increasingly out of control in the process. She is like a cat without a righting reflex, that inner mechanism cats depend on when they fall upside down from a tree and land on their feet. Without an intact method of regaining her footing, Stacy's "optimism" depends on not getting her upbeat mood shaken, on never falling upside down from six stories. She can't possibly be truly optimistic about the future, because she knows that at any time she could enter a mood tailspin from which she would have difficulty recovering.

I've heard a similar concern about becoming a bag lady from so many people who can't pull themselves out of their own psychological free falls that I've come to believe it's a metaphor for their poverty of control over their own inner states, a description of the depths to which their moods can plunge. To make matters worse, when I asked my friend what triggers these bouts of self-doubt and worry, she had no idea. That means she feels chronically at risk of being thrown for a loop and constantly concerned about her ability to right herself once she is thrown, but she has no idea how to anticipate what will trigger her disastrous fall. She has to be on guard all the time, and she spends a good deal of psychic energy trying to keep her mood good, to convince herself and others that she is feeling optimistic. In addition, chances are she feels her positive upbeat self-presentation is essentially false, not true to who she really is. So an added problem of her mood-regulation style is likely to be that she feels like a fake, a self-perspective that may also contribute to her bag lady fantasies.

Vicky's seemingly self-defeating attempts to bring herself down a notch when she feels a little too good suggests that mood modulation is important even when what we are regulating is a *positive* state of mind. In the face of her success at work, she becomes intensely excited. You'd expect her at this moment to feel confident about the future and optimistic about her prospects. Instead she worries about a small error in a memo and blows it all out of proportion. Why? Her intense excitement feels uncomfortable to her, too much, too overwhelming, too likely to make her too full of herself and too grandiose. Like my friend the lawyer, she fears being out of control, but in the opposite direction. Instead of falling six stories and landing on her head, she's more worried that amid an intense and uncomfortably excited feeling state she'll simply take off and fly around the room, psychologically speaking. She worries in order to bring her mood back down a notch, into more comfortable territory where she feels in control of herself. This kind of psychological deflation does work, but it is a poor way of modulating inner emotions, because it limits the excitement she can let herself feel in a situation, such as a promotion, where feeling excited and even joyful would be entirely appropriate. It'd be better if she could expand her capacity for tolerating intense excitement instead. Then she could enjoy her own successes without the fear of being emotionally over the top and having to reign herself in.

This is not to say that the goal of mood modulation is to keep us in an emotionally comfortable, positive place all the time any more than the goal of modulation in music is to always keep us singing in C major. To do so would make our worlds dull and uninteresting. There are reasons that some of us seek out the intense mixture of fear and excitement generated by those amusement park rides and horror flicks, why others purposefully watch reruns of *Love Story* on TV even though they know they'll cry. What we tend to think of as negative mood states—anxiety, sadness, and the like—do not always make us pessimistic when we feel at the helm of them. In fact, proving to ourselves that we can handle fear or sadness—even master it—is probably part of the appeal of leisure activities that generate strong feelings. The real key is control and choice. When these negative feelings wash over us in unbidden waves and threaten to swamp us, then they become problematic. Positive feelings can become uncomfortable in this way, too, when they seem too intense for us to handle. As in music, tension, dissonance, and heightened intensity in our moods make life interesting. When we know we have the capacity to compose ourselves effectively, we also have a wider range of feelings that seem comfortable, familiar, and acceptable to us. With this wider range of emotional timbres available, we have more access to our inner fantasy lives and creativity as well.

Like composers choosing to work in a difficult key, we are more comfortable moving into those challenging mood states at the edges of our control when we know that we have the inner skills and know the steps to bring ourselves back out of them again. The better we are at it and the more in charge we feel, the more risks we can take. Doing so depends on our sense that we will be able to get back from the somber dark perspectives without getting stuck in them. A life lived only in primary colors is like a piece of music that lacks tension and dissonance: overly bright and brassy with no creeping bass line. It is like giving up the grays, deep blues, browns, and blacks from our emotional palette. Although we wouldn't want to live forever inside a Sousa march, we also wouldn't want to trade it in for a perpetual fugue. Most people don't want to be purely pastel Impressionists or Pollyannaish optimists, nor do they want to wind up as permanently pessimistic Rembrandts, either. The best perspective to have from the standpoint of psychological health is a flexible one that allows us use of the entire palette with skills for deciding what styles and colors to use in different situations.

Kay Redfield Jamison, a psychiatrist who suffers from manic depression, describes the inevitable ebb and flow of her moods and the optimism and pessimism that accompanies them like this:

> We all build internal sea walls to keep at bay the sadnesses of life and the often overwhelming forces within our own minds....One of the most difficult problems is to construct these barriers of such a height and strength that one has a true harbor, a sanctuary away from crippling turmoil and

pain but low enough, and permeable enough, to let in fresh seawater that will fend off the inevitable inclination toward brackishness.[5]

The challenge is to allow ourselves to feel and feel deeply, avoiding the brackishness that shallow and stunted feelings produce, without being overwhelmed by the sadness, pain, and turmoil that experiencing our inner feelings can bring when they are too intense for us to handle.

While pessimists can sing only a single note, their own anxiety echoing around them, optimists are masterful mental musicians who have been able to construct such permeable barriers that regulate the intensity and range of inner feeling states without quashing their feelings. More important to sustaining their optimistic stance, though, is the fact that they know they can rely on themselves to have what they need inside, no matter what life dishes out. Like the canal man who regulates a complex lock and dam system with ease, they know that they can control the ebb and flow of their inner feeling states, that they are at the helm. This self-sufficiency and capacity for autonomy based on their emotional abilities makes optimists resilient, gives them the outer shell—and the inner skills—needed to make it through tough times. In contrast, pessimists are less fortunate and less skilled at managing their own inner states. The more time they spend in problematic mood states, such as anxiety, the more pessimistic they are.[6]

Optimism is derived from the Latin word *optimus,* meaning "best." Originally, it was the name given to the doctrine propounded by the philosopher Leibniz, in his 1710 work *Théodicée,* which asserted that the actual world is the "best of all possible worlds." Leibniz believed that the world in which we live was chosen by the Creator out of all the possible worlds present in his thoughts, as the world in which the most good could be obtained at the cost of the least evil. If we recast optimism in the inner terms I suggest, this old definition still holds. Optimism arises when our actual inner world is the best of all possible inner worlds at a given moment—the world that maximizes our comfort and sense of autonomous control.

My new view of optimism contains the fundamental good news that our modulating of the moods that color our inner world doesn't depend on our external circumstances. But we already know that anyway, don't we? Sure, we admire people who are able to remain optimistic even in the face of dramatic and difficult external circumstances or futures that seem less than bright. And we know the corollary, that the richest among us who are surrounded by luxury and have future prospects that seem glittering are sometimes also the most pessimistic and hopeless about their plights. In the past we've thought of these perspectives on the world as genetically determined aspects of personality. But given the extent to which our perspectives depend on our mood at any given moment, doesn't it make more sense to believe that in order to feel in control, cheerful, and optimistic, we need to recognize that the only gorillas that can really tear us apart are those that attack us from within? Feeling optimistic is a reflection of our belief in and experience of our own capacity for the self-regulation of emotional states, especially painful, negative ones. The stronger this inner capacity for self-regulation, for achieving emotional comfort and self-soothing in the midst of a crisis, the greater our sense of optimism. An inner sense of autonomy, self-reliance, and integrated personhood are the real inner islands of strength that optimists possess and from which they spin the illusions that sustain and buoy them when the going gets rough. This strength allows them to do remarkable things, like the musicians on the *Titanic* who played while the ship sank, neither minimizing the very real danger that they faced nor succumbing to inner terror.

Optimism depends on seeing the self as full of the emotional stuff it takes to rise to challenges and weather life's storms. Optimists believe that they are robust, and this perspective in turn allows them to choose to see the glass as half full rather than half empty. How well and smoothly our emotional regulation works will determine how much of our daily lives we spend in this optimistic, comfortable state. The more time we spend in this state, the more we will look like an optimist. But appearing optimistic merely reflects the aggregate, the sum of those little oscillating moments of optimism and pessimism over time, not some stable, enduring, unshakable trait. And that's good news, because it means that even small shifts in our capacity for self-regulation can lead to large differences in how much of our day we spend in a comfortable, peaceful emotional state.

But the strength of mood-congruence effects also means that when in a sad mood, we will tend to think sad thoughts, seek out stimuli (such as a sad song on the radio) that match that mood, and see ourselves and others in light of our current inner state. In order to modulate our mood from sadness to an upbeat emotional climate, we have to work against these mood-congruence effects. In other words, we have to find a way to alter our mood,

perhaps by thinking happy thoughts or seeking upbeat sensations or finding cheerful perspectives on
ourselves and others to help pull ourselves out of our
sad state of mind. But our sad state of mind tugs at
our thoughts and perceptions, trying to bring them
back in line with our mood. Our inner mood state is
convincing, and we believe its perspective of ourselves, others, and the versions of the past and future
that it portrays, so we are often unable or unwilling
to really question our perspective. Mood modulation
from a sad or anxious or angry feeling state requires,
in essence, that we take our mood seriously enough
to try to pull ourselves out of it, but not seriously
enough to see it as an accurate reflection of reality.
Reminding my patients that their vision of the
world, themselves, and those around them is colored
by their current mood is one of my most frequent interventions as a psychiatrist, and an extremely difficult lesson for them to learn.

The impact of what happens in the world around
us upon how we feel is undeniable. When gorillas
break out of their cages, of course it makes us anxious. But it is crucial to the task of becoming more
optimistic that we not underestimate the pivotal role
our current inner state plays in shaping how we see
that world. Anxiety can make us feel out of control

and beastly, causing us to imagine that gorillas abound all around us even when the coast is clear. This notion is captured in the old psychoanalytic joke that I remembered when Vicky first told me about her dream. A woman dreams that she's being chased by a gorilla, and she runs in terror as the gorilla closes in. He gets closer and closer until finally the woman can feel his warm breath on her neck. "Well, now that you've caught me, what are you going to do with me?" the lady asks in a quavering voice. "I don't know, lady," replies the gorilla. "After all, this is *your* dream."

Chapter Three

IN THE DRIVER'S SEAT

ONE SIMPLE CONCLUSION you might draw from what I've just said about the crucial connection between positive emotional states and optimism is that you should find what you love to do, what makes you excited and happy, and do it. When you're feeling happy, excited, and interested, your perspective on your past, present, and future is likely to be most optimistic. Of course, because mood congruence is such a powerful phenomenon, pulling ourselves out of negative emotions means working against our tendency to believe that they are accurate perspectives on the world around us. That means that finding what they love to do and doing it doesn't always come easily to people caught in the grip of anger, anxiety, and sadness, no matter how simple it sounds. But when it's possible, it can be the surest route to a more optimistic stance.

As for me, I've learned that I'm rarely as happy as when I'm driving, zipping along the West Side Highway with the radio blaring, singing songs I like, at the top of my lungs. Perhaps it's the sense I have of hugging the rim of Manhattan, skating along the island's edge without falling off. Or maybe it's a stubborn vestige of my Texan roots, growing up as I did in a culture where cars symbolize freedom and mobility rather than the traffic jams and parking frustrations that most New Yorkers tend to associate with them. Truth be told, when I drive I often go a bit too fast and sing a bit too loud. It probably feels so good because I have the sense that I am the master of my own little universe, regulating my speed, my destination, the route I will take, and what I will see and hear and sing along the way. I feel optimistic.

Recently a new series of billboards began to push their way into my awareness. Things like "Half of the drivers in New York State flunked their driver's test the first time around. Be careful." And "Forty percent of drivers are busy reading this billboard instead of watching the road." (You can see that I am among them.) Of course, the ads were supposed to be attention grabbing, humorous. But they did make me think twice as well. It wasn't that *I* was out of control, understand, but the ads did suggest that the people all around me might be. Maybe, I allowed cautiously, there were even moments where I was pushing the envelope too much myself.

Optimism depends on being able to sustain a sense of control and to enjoy the illusion that we're in the driver's seat even though it's really just an illusion. It comes from feeling that we control our destiny even though there's evidence all around us to the contrary. There is a reciprocal relationship between this capacity to experience a sense of control and mastery of the world around us and our ability to wrestle the gorillas within into submission. Our sense of being in the driver's seat when it comes to taming our own emotions allows us to feel in control of the world around us and vice versa. But this link between a sense of outer control and calming what's within is not just circular. Rather, I see it as a spiral, and when you're a patient in the throes of depression, that's a subtle but important distinction. In therapy sessions the patients and I often trace how their inner anxieties tend to make them see troubles all around, and how that in turn is sure to make them sink further into descending spirals of anxiety. But, I hope to show them that, given a boost in the right direction, they might muster enough inner strength to see hope on the horizon, assume the driver's seat, and effect a reciprocal positive cycle. And the greater our sense of control over the world around us, even if that sense of control is really an illusion, the greater our capacity for optimism.

In fact, it turns out that we like to feel in control so much that we will create the illusion of being in the driver's seat even when we're really Lady Luck's passenger instead. It's a fascinating phenomenon: people playing games that are based entirely on chance can often make themselves and bystanders believe that they control what are actually random events.[1] For instance, in one study, gamblers who threw the dice slowly when they wanted a low number and swiftly when they wanted a high number convinced bystanders that they could actually exert an influence on the outcome of the roll. In fact, when you introduce the elements of competition ("Let's see who can throw the lowest roll"), choice ("Pick a card, any card, from the deck"), and strategy ("I need a six to win the backgammon game") into what is really a random-chance game, people who should know better will begin to believe that what is chancy at best involves skill and control rather than luck. Observers even become more willing to wager larger amounts of money when these elements that heighten the illusion of control on the part of the player are visibly present, and they are more confident that the players can roll the exact number they need again.[2]

When a player really needs a given outcome—such as hungry people given a chance to win hamburgers in random drawings—those who are hungriest will also be the most confident of drawing the winning (random) card from a deck and will think there is more skill involved in doing so.[3] We want our actions to matter so much that we can even convince ourselves we can seduce Lady Luck into letting us drive after all. When we really need a given outcome, we want to believe in the illusion of control so badly we can taste it. After all, how would we feel about living in a universe that is truly indifferent to our fervent desire for a Big Mac, a world that won't let us have our way?

This example highlights why our brains may be built to look for evidence that we're in the driver's seat even when we're not: believing that we're calling the shots helps buffer us against the flood of negative feelings—depression, anxiety, anger, and despair—that might arise if we were to confront our true helplessness. This connection between the ability to maintain the illusion of control and the capacity to sustain a positive mood is a powerful one. For example, in one study, the more subjects were convinced that they exerted control over the random appearance of a lighted square on a computer screen, the less likely they were to succumb to a negative mood when asked to solve unsolvable anagrams (designed by creative but sadistic researchers in order to create feelings of helplessness and failure in their subjects). Their counterparts, who estimated that they exerted less control over the square, were much more easily demoralized in the face of failure and became anxious and depressed in response. Furthermore, subjects who were the most convinced that they controlled the really random square were less likely to have become discouraged even in the face of high amounts of real-life adversity in the month preceding the study than their compatriots, who spent less time feeling happy and more time feeling anxious and depressed, even when they had experienced fewer real-life stressors.[4] In other words, believing we are in control clearly contributes to our ability to sustain a robustly positive mood and outlook, even though that sense of control is only an illusion. In contrast to what decades of mental health professionals have thought about the importance of having a firm grip on reality, our illusions of control foster positive states of mind even though they are really distortions of the "truth."

It even seems that we are capable of adjusting our beliefs about reality quite specifically in order to psychologically protect ourselves and buffer ourselves against negative feelings. When asked how anxious they were about various bad events as well as how likely it was that those bad events would befall them, subjects in one study said that the events they were the most worried about were the least likely to happen. So those who were the most concerned about contracting AIDS also said it was less likely to happen to them than things they were less worried about, such as car accidents or losing their jobs.[5] In fact, this effect was so robust that gay men who were HIV positive but healthy (and thus presumably more anxious about actually developing AIDS) rated themselves as less likely to develop AIDS than did other healthy gay men who were HIV negative!

Indeed, creating the illusion of control works well in modulating negative mood states, even in people with rather extreme levels of anxiety. In one study, twenty patients with panic attacks breathed the same amount of carbon dioxide-rich air (which precipitates panic symptoms). But half believed they could always control how much of the air they breathed, while the other half believed they never had control over the amount. In the end, fully 80% of those who thought they had no control over the air flow had panic attacks, while only 20% of those who had the illusion of controlling their air intake did, even though both groups breathed the very same amount of panic-inducing air in the end. The belief that we can control the world around us can actually translate into very real control over our negative feelings and a corresponding increase in our level of optimism.[6]

You might have three nagging concerns as I tell you about the importance of the illusion of control and its link to optimism. First of all, you might think that even if it fosters resiliency and positive moods, buying into illusions amounts to engaging in the kind of wishful thinking that would make us less likely to see what our problems are and tackle them head on. For instance, if the idea of having a heart attack makes us anxious and we come to believe it won't happen to us, does that mean we will fail to take the very steps—such as changing our diet or exercising more—that would actually head off a heart attack? In other words, will we fail to address and change things we really have control over simply because we want to sustain the illusion that they are not problems? This has not generally proved to be the case when this issue has been studied, with several important exceptions. First, there are some gamblers whose belief in the illusion of control gets them into trouble and keeps them coming back for more, unable to admit that they are not really the rulers of the roulette wheel after all. There is also some evidence that teenage girls who have more illusions of control about getting pregnant may fail to use birth control with regularity. But there's more evidence going in the opposite direction: people who have an intact illusion of control are more likely to be proactive in addressing real problems, whereas those who lack the illusion of being in the driver's seat often resort to avoidance.[7] This makes sense because, of course, an intact illusion of control is also related to the belief that your actions matter. So when you see a problem, you're more likely to believe you can solve it. This is why pessimists, who believe that their car is more likely to crash, are actually less likely to be wearing their seat belts when it does. Their high levels of anxiety and sense of hopelessness translate into inaction, whereas the more upbeat emotions of their optimistic counterparts tend to make them believe what they do makes a difference, encouraging them to take action.

A second concern you might have about succumbing to an illusion of control is that you may worry about what will happen when that illusion is actually shattered. After all, life continually confronts us with evidence that we're not really in the driver's seat. And if we buy into the illusion that we are, won't we be more disappointed and more disillusioned when the unthinkable happens and we actually crash? Won't reality be even more disturbing when our illusions of control are shattered than it would have been if we didn't believe we had control in the first place? The answer, simply put, is no. In breast cancer patients, those who were not depressed asserted that they had high degrees of personal control over the recurrence of their cancer. But when confronted with the bad news that their cancer had in fact returned, the patients still did not give up the illusion that they had control. They merely shifted what they thought they had control of. So instead of believing they could prevent a relapse, they instead began to focus on controlling their own medical treatment, creating the illusion that they were calling the shots about other things. By narrowing their ambitions about what was in their control in the face of a relapse, they were able to continue to believe the illusion. Their adjustment was rated by themselves,

psychologists, family members, and their cancer doc-
tors to be better than patients whose illusions were
shattered, patients with recurrent breast cancer who
were depressed. Furthermore, the women who sustained the illusion of being at the helm had less pain,
lived longer, and enjoyed themselves more as compared to the depressed and demoralized cancer patients who felt the cancer was beyond their control.
In other words, the illusion of control fosters positive
inner processes, and these inner processes can actually give us real control over what happens to us in
the end. The illusion of control is in part a self-
fulfilling prophecy. The breast cancer patients with
the illusion of control were more optimistic about
their prospects, and in the end they did really have
more reason to be optimistic than their more pessimistic cohorts.[8]

A third issue about the mood and illusion-of-
control connection is that you may be wondering
which way the arrows of influence go. Does the illusion of control sustain an upbeat mood that makes
optimism possible? Or does an upbeat mood itself
make possible the illusion of being at the helm? It
turns out that there is a reciprocal and constantly
reverberating relationship between the two. When
otherwise healthy people are made sad or anxious by

listening to sad music or anxiety-provoking stories, they actually temporarily lose part of their ability to construct an illusion of control. And when depressed people have their mood temporarily elevated by watching a funny film, they become better able to sustain the illusion that they are in control as well as more likely to underestimate their chances of having a wide variety of bad things happen to them, at least for the moment.[9] Sustaining the illusion is important to maintaining some sense of control over our inner emotional world, and this control in turn helps us to sustain the illusion that we are in the driver's seat, which then buoys our mood. Talk about potential for upward and downward spirals! Yet feeling happy is related to a generalized sense of feeling in control in daily life.[10]

Taking the question of the relationship between emotions and the illusion of control a step further, real-life experiences of loss of control are clearly a major determinant of how effective our ability to sustain positive illusions and upbeat moods will be in later life. But the manner in which this important relationship became clear was, like so many other important scientific discoveries, accidental and seren-dipitous.

If anyone would feel they're in control, you'd

think it would be scientific researchers. After all, their job is to control and manipulate things in order to study them. And indeed, the first two parts of the planned study were supposed to be simple. First, the dogs were to be exposed to two types of stimuli: a high-pitched tone then a brief shock to the paws when the metal floor of their cages were momentarily mildly electrified. They were supposed to be learning to fear the tone, associating it with the shock. An example of Pavlov 101. In part two they were supposed to learn to jump over a low wall between two compartments to escape the shock, leaping to the other side of the cage with its insulated floor in order to protect their paws. The big step was supposed to be part three, when the researchers would see if the dogs would leap the wall in response to the tone alone. In other words, could they put together the two pieces of information they had learned (tone means a shock is coming and the shock can be escaped by jumping) to form a novel response: tone means jump.

The proposed study was not to be, however, because after the tone and the shock were repeatedly paired in part one and the researchers went on to part two, the dogs simply lay down in their cages and whimpered when the shock was turned on. They didn't try to escape even though relief was but a small leap away. No one could even begin to see if they would leap the wall in response to the tone, because they wouldn't even jump it in response to the shock. While the other researchers were peeved by this interruption of their research plan, psychologist Martin Seligman saw the dogs' responses as a serendipitous event that would let him study the anatomy of despair.[11] As he thought about what had happened to the dogs, he reasoned that the key to their response was that the first part of the study, in which the tone and shock were paired, had taught the dogs that they were helpless. No matter what they did, the shock went on and off in a way that they could not control. They had concluded that their actions didn't make a difference. So even though they could have controlled the shock in part two by leaping over the low wall, they didn't even try because they didn't expect anything they did to matter anyway. By learning that they were helpless to control their fate, they had been reduced to a whimper, the essence of pessimism.

Seligman began to explore more systematically the phenomenon he calls learned helplessness. This time he took three groups of dogs and gave one group shocks from which the dogs could escape by pushing a panel with their noses. The second group was given shocks that they could not escape, no matter what they did. And the last group received no shocks at all. Dogs in the first and second groups were "yoked" to control the total amount of shock they received; the second dogs (who could not influence the shocks) were shocked only as long as it took their partner dogs from the first group to escape the shocks. (So if you were a group two pooch, you'd better hope your canine compatriot in group one learned new tricks quickly!) This yoking was used to demonstrate that it was not just the overall amount of shock that led to helplessness, because the dogs in the first two groups were shocked for exactly the same amount of time. All three groups of dogs were next tested in the cage with the low wall, in which one compartment was electrified and the other was not.

The dogs from the first group, who had been able to escape the shocks in the previous part of the study, and the dogs that had never been shocked, quickly learned to jump the barrier and escape the shock. But the dogs in the second group, who had learned that nothing they did mattered and that they could not escape the shock, merely sat down in the compartments and waited for the shock to end. They never learned to jump into the other compartment and escape the shock; in fact, like the dogs that paralyzed the experimental process in the original study, they never even tried. They had concluded that they were helpless, the situation hopeless, and they acted resigned to their fates. They had constructed an inner picture of themselves in the world in which they were out of control. Their level of positive expectations about their ability to make an impact plummeted accordingly. Furthermore, their sense that they lacked control persisted even when the reality of the situation shifted and they could have remedied their situation.

Dogs with earlier experiences that led them to construct a vision of a world in which they had no control acted in accord with this negative perspective even later, when it really was an illusion. In contrast, puppies who were systematically trained in early life to believe their actions mattered sustained the illusion of control longer when they were really helpless in later life. If as puppies they had been "immunized" against helplessness by participating in situations such as learning to escape shocks, it took them much longer to get discouraged than dogs who had no such illusion of control to begin with. In other words, it is the perception of being in control, not the reality, that really matters. Learning whether or not what you do makes an impact and acting in accord with this belief in later life—even if it is an illusion given your current reality—is a robust phenomenon. So robust, in fact, that even lowly cockroaches with their tiny insect brains exhibit learned helplessness.[12] They are bugged to discover what they do has no impact.

Furthermore, the learned helplessness paradigm is still used to create miserable creatures, such as depressed dogs on whom new antidepressant drugs are tested! And the loss of control–negative emotion connection is a powerful one in people as well. When researchers produce learned helplessness by giving people no control over loud noises, one thing that reliably happens is that their subjects become anxious, depressed, and angry. These negative feelings are also accompanied by increased release of stress hormones, such as cortisol and adrenaline, which take a toll on everything from our moods to our immune systems. The physical changes that being helpless in the face of loud noises produce are even greater in people who already have a history of depression, suggesting that they are particularly susceptible to a sense of loss of control. It is as if their systems are already primed from prior life experience to respond to situations in which they are helpless to control the world around them.[13]

The outer control–inner emotion equation goes

beyond the link between loss of control and depression. Just as being in control of a bad event like a shock to the paws mitigates how it affects us, literally making it have less impact, possessing or lacking control over good events also affects how much we enjoy them. In one study, two-month-old babies were placed in infant seats. One group of babies had strings tied to their arms that turned on a short snatch of music when pulled. The other group had a similar set of strings attached, but pulling the strings did nothing. Instead, music came on and off at random. The researchers found much higher levels of interest, smiling, and engagement among babies in the first group, while babies in the second group remained blasé, not reacting much to the music that surrounded them.[14]

The take-home message is that from the very beginning of life we are delighted to learn that what we do makes a difference. And when we feel in control, we enjoy the things that resulted from our own actions more fully than if they just happen without any input from us. Even babies like to pull the strings and see the puppets dance. No one prefers events, whether good or bad, to be beyond our control. Lacking control over shocks is bad, but even lacking control over good things like music makes them less pleasant and enjoyable.

The good news about the link between inner emotion and outer control is that you can teach an old dog—even a depressed, demoralized one—new tricks. In the end, Seligman taught his helpless hounds a new move. He dragged each pathetically helpless pooch over the low wall between the compartment that was electrified and the one that was not until the dogs got it. "Eureka!" they may have thought as they finally realized they could avoid the shock by jumping the wall. They realized that they did have some control over the situation and that their actions mattered. Once they learned that they were not really helpless, the dogs were depressed and passive no more, leaping tall barriers in a single bound. Knowing that what they did made a difference brought them from pessimistic underdogs who could only lie and whine to optimistic superdogs that were able to take charge of protecting their own paws in a pinch. Regaining a sense of our ability to make an impact bolsters our moods, in the process permitting us the more optimistic stance that the positive moods and our sense of autonomy and self-regulation make possible. These more positive emotional states then further boost our sense that we are in the driver's seat.

For me, one sure cure for a depressed or angry or anxious mood and the pessimistic ruminations that accompany it is to get out on the highway and go for a drive. It's a way of feeling in control and powerful, able to have an impact and to find my own road; and the illusion of control that it helps to foster bolsters my sense of being able to autonomously regulate my own inner states. Perhaps it's not called a "self-mobile" for nothing. It turns out that I'm not the only one who feels this way about driving, since at least one study about illusions of control showed that almost everyone rates themselves as a better than average driver who is less likely than most to crash. Since we can't all be in the upper 50%, there must be something about being behind the wheel that in and of itself fosters the illusion of control and the optimism that accompanies it. Jean Cocteau understood this phenomenon when he said that a car can massage organs no masseur can reach. He called driving the one remedy for disorders of the sympathetic nervous system, the one that was sent spinning out of control in the experiment I described where subjects learned that they were helpless to control a loud and annoying noise and responded with increased cortisol and adrenaline. Somehow, almost without fail, I find my mood lifting and my spirit soaring when I'm behind the wheel, cruising along, singing, and, admittedly, speeding. Like a turtle I carry with me whatever I need to feel at home as I travel about in the world. My car and the illusion it allows me to create about being in charge in the world are truly a protective carapace. When driving I feel I can rely on myself to have what I need to handle whatever life dishes out, see the half-empty gas tank as half full instead.

Contrast this with myself at other, less fortunate times, when I have less of a sense of controlling what's happening around me and therefore also less capacity to manage my own inner states. Succumbing to depressive realism, I am instead traveling through life with the monkeys of anxiety, depression, and anger on my back in lieu of my own mobile home. But over time I have become better at shaking these monkeys and replacing them with the illusions that sustain optimism instead. It's lucky that we can all expand with practice our capacity for self-regulation of our inner states, because we all deserve a taste of the autonomy that comes from feeling in charge of ourselves, finding our own roads, and choosing our own destinations. As we've seen, this sense of control is partly illusory, but even so, it is an illusion that ultimately makes a real difference. And the illusion of control and the increased capacity for mood regulation that it brings also enable us to feel more optimistic from moment to moment, more able to enjoy the feeling of the wind whipping through our hair as we zip along through life.

Chapter Four

VITAL
LIMBIC LESSONS

THE RESEARCH ON learned helplessness presented
in the last chapter suggests that the reciprocal connections between the capacity to maintain the illusion of control, positive inner emotions, and
optimism arises from early life experiences in which
the *real* ability to make an impact on the world was
either fostered or thwarted. At least that's the story
for dogs. But what about people? What is it in our
early life experience that either puts us in the driver's
seat or makes us feel as if we are merely passengers on
an out-of-control roller coaster of emotions? In this
chapter we'll take a look at what kind of early life
experiences positively or adversely affect our later

capacity for mood modulation and the optimistic perspective that accompanies it.

If you've ever watched a baby dissolve into a storm of sobs, screams, and tears, you'll appreciate the fact that whether the inner gorillas with which we must wrestle from the very beginning of life arise from hunger, a wet diaper, or from the anxiety that separation from a caretaker can produce, they can be formidable opponents, easily overwhelming and dys-regulating us. Early in life we have only the rudimen-tary beginnings of an evolving ability to modulate our states of mind. We are basically helpless, in terms of both our ability to have an effect on the world around us and our ability to control the tempest in-side. Our parents or other important caretakers are our comforters; they can help us make our way out of emotionally difficult states, both taking charge for us when we are upset and then gradually helping us to take control for ourselves. Simply put, caretakers are the ones who ultimately teach us the tricks of the trade when it comes to heightening happiness or at-tenuating anger, the secrets and shortcuts through which to modulate our inner moods. As Myron Hofer, a psychiatrist and attachment researcher puts it, "the caretaker literally serves as an external regula-tor of the structure and neurochemistry of the child's maturing brain."[1] In other words, optimism's circuitry is established, ultimately etched into the neurons of our brains, according to the lessons that our early life experiences with caretakers give our limbic systems, the parts of our brains responsible for emotional responses. These experiences give us the methods and the pathways through which we attempt to modulate our emotional responses for the rest of our lives. So by looking at what happens under ideal circumstances—as well as what can go wrong—we can understand how optimism and pessimism arise. Although any important caretaker probably fills this bill, most of the studies I will describe were conducted with mothers, and I will use this word—*mothers*—throughout, both to be accurate in describing research findings and as shorthand for "parents" or "fathers" or "caretakers." In a very real sense, the moment-to-moment modulation of a child's inner state by a caretaker accompanied by the gradual transfer of this capacity for self-regulation to the child is the central task of parenting.

At the center of our efforts to regulate emotion is an unimpressive-looking piece of brain that resembles a nut. A small almond, to be precise. The aptly named amygdala (which means "almond" in Latin) is the site of attacks of fear and rage as well as a card-carrying member of the limbic system, the portion of the brain most closely associated with emotion. Intense emotions happen when the limbic system is all fired up about something, when the nerve cells that comprise it are hopping. So it is our two little almonds (one on each side of the brain) and the rest of the limbic system (such as the anterior cingulate cortex) that surrounds them that we seek to influence when we attempt to make our brains function in a more optimistic manner. The limbic system is centrally positioned to affect both our bodies and our brains. It sends information via nerves directly to our bodies' muscles and internal organs, and it also affects the body indirectly via hormonal messages (by triggering a brain center called the hypothalamus to release into the blood chemicals that affect our endocrine or hormone systems). These bodily effects of various emotional states are then reflected back to the rest of the brain as inputs. In other words, being afraid might cause our skeletal muscles to tense, then this tension is reflected back to our brains and probably helps contribute to the feeling of fear. In addition, the limbic system "talks" to the areas in the brain stem below it that contain the clusters of nerve cells that release dopamine, norepinephrine, and serotonin. These neurotransmitters in turn have a far-reaching and profound modulatory effect on the way the rest of the brain, especially the cortex, operates. They are the chemicals influenced by antidepressant medications, and they are crucial to the cortex because in effect they establish cortical weather conditions, determining the environment in which the neurons that underlie our thought processes will operate. The limbic system is central and powerful, both helping to produce the bodily effects associated with emotions, such as the racing heart of fear, as well as affecting the chemical climate in which the rest of the brain operates when under the influence of a given emotion.

The amygdala can nonetheless be a tough nut to crack. Its centrality means that it stands like a sentinel, sandwiched between a stream of information, bubbling up from the body and lower brain areas, about what's happening both inside and outside the body and the constant chatter of the cortex above. The lower brain runs incoming sensory information by the limbic system so that it can look for emotionally relevant cues and clues. The cortex depends on the amygdala's emotionally sensitive input to inform the timbre of its otherwise cold, hard, reasonable talk.[2] Our cortex—which is responsible for our brains being over two and a half times as large as our nearest chimpanzee competitors—takes the emotional information the limbic system provides and elaborates and refines it, turning limbic lust, for example, into the more complicated cortical love. Because the cortex has six layers and the possibility for many interconnections, it processes information in a sophisticated and subtle way, even allowing us to have thoughts about our thoughts and feelings, giving rise to consciousness and our capacity for self-reflection. Although even our species name *Homo sapiens* focuses on our cortical ability for sapience—our ability to know—our limbic system is of central importance when it comes to optimism and pessimism.

As with other kinds of learning, what we need first is to be calm and comfortable enough to attend to what the teacher is saying. That's why our mother's first task as our brain trainer is essentially to pacify us, to put us into a state in which we can learn the lessons that will follow. She uses tactics like rocking, stroking, cuddling, and cooing as well as feeding, bathing, and changing us to calm us and to make our inner state and physical self more comfortable. All these interventions have the effect of sending soothing sensations from our bodies and the world outside into the stream of information that the limbic system, especially the amygdala, is constantly evaluating. Bathed in a calming incoming stream of sensation, the limbic system gradually allows itself to be lulled into a more quiet state that permits the emotion of contented interest to prevail. While we may not yet be able to control ourselves, if our mothers are responsive to our needs, then we learn that it is possible to quell the tempest of unpleasant sensations within. Once a baby is in a state of contented interest, then limbic limbo lessons can begin in earnest as a mother seeks to stretch the bounds of her baby's capacity for upbeat emotions. But in this case the real question is not "how low can you go?" but how high. Inducing and amplifying positive feelings in babies can happen in many ways, but one of the most predictable and intense occurs when infants look into their mother's eyes like lovers, allowing the process of gazing to trigger the upward spirals of pleasure in one another that induce a sense of contented connectedness and joy.[3] The mother senses the baby's affective state, meets and matches his mood where it is at the moment, then nudges the baby's mood into a slightly more expansive, joyful place by conveying a slightly broader positive response. Her goal is to push the envelope, to encourage the infant to go right up to the edge, when it comes to the intensity of feeling he can tolerate without pushing him beyond, into a place where the positive feeling seems overwhelming instead. If you've ever closely observed the seemingly infectious nature of smiles between parents and their infants that end with both chuckling, you've watched this positive spiral in action.

But the beginnings of control—including control over one's own inner reactions and over the intensity of the interpersonal experience with Mom—are potentially present from earliest infancy as well. The baby can control the intense inner experience that interactions like gazing into the mother's eyes induces by looking away, momentarily stopping the incoming sensations from Mom and putting the brakes on the powerful surge of positive feelings that gazing evokes. Looking away is one of the baby's first tactics for self-modulation, immediately limiting the sensory bombardment (albeit positive stimulation) that the mother's smiling face represents and allowing his increasingly stimulated limbic system to take a break before returning for more. Babies tend to have accelerations in their heart rates five seconds before they choose to look away, suggesting that they avert their eyes just as they're getting physiologically overstimulated, entering a zone in which continued stimulation would be uncomfortable and disorganizing, sending the baby spiraling over the top. And by look-

ing away herself, the mother can control the intensity
with which she stimulates her baby. Thus she can
prevent the surge of positive emotion from continuing to escalate until the infant is disorganized and
overwhelmed, spinning out of control. In this manner she can gradually push the infant to tolerate more
and more positive stimulation one notch at a time,
slowly expanding the range of positive emotion he
can comfortably tolerate.[4]

The job of modulating an infant's emotions is a
tricky one, since infant's emotional states are very
sloppy, sliding from one to another like a trombone
player with a lazy arm. Infants quickly go from crying and upset to asleep. Elation rapidly slides across
the line from intense pleasure into disorganization. It
is as if we are born with so little control over our inner states that our mothers can play us like musical
instruments. We are malleable in early life, and these
early interactions will set the mold for the development of our emotional palettes and patterns.

Over time and with practice, the intensity levels
of positive feelings like happiness and elation that babies can tolerate grow gradually greater as their mothers continually stretch and expand the outer limits of
positive feeling that the infant perceives as comfortable rather than disorganizing. This repeated positive

amplification of the infant's emotions has been linked to the development of the orbitofrontal cortex in the brain's right hemisphere. This brain area is developing during the first year of life as neurons grow up into it from the lower limbic system and the cortex sends neurons back down to the limbic system in return. In other words, as all this positive amplification is occurring between mothers and their babies, a loop between cortex and limbic system is also developing, creating the neural circuitry that the baby will use to control and manage positive feelings. These neuronal connections from the limbic system to the cortex are powered by the neurotransmitter dopamine, which is known to be important in pleasure- and reward-seeking behaviors throughout life. In fact, it is the rewarding feelings of elation, calm, and well-being these early life interactions evoke that many drug users seem to be seeking when they choose to use one of the many drugs that increase dopamine. The elevated level of dopaminergic stimulation in this first cortico-limbic pathway that arises from interactions like long, soulful gazing at Mom leads to the emotional states of interest, excitement, and joy so commonly seen in the first few months of life.[5]

In fact, the development of this first cortico-limbic loop of our optimism circuitry during the first year coincides with a time of life in which about 90% of all caretaker–child interactions are affectionate, caregiving, or playful situations characterized by the caretaker amplifying and sharing positive affects.[6] Once formed, the cortico-limbic circuit allows the child to experience and to begin to learn to regulate positive affects, such as elation, for himself.

Just what is happening in the orbitofrontal cortex that allows it ultimately to exert control over the limbic system anyway? The right orbitofrontal cortex's job is probably to store information developing in the cortex about how certain representations or mental pictures of ourselves and those around us are paired with certain feeling states. In other words, the orbitofrontal cortex, to which the limbic system neurons are attached, provides a crucial neuronal link to the psychological portraits of ourselves in a happy state and our mothers in a positive or encouraging state, which all those positive interactions are helping to paint. Psychoanalytic theory suggests that when we take in relationships and encode them in our brains, we internalize them in bite-sized nuggets that consist of a portrait of ourselves and a portrait of the other person plus the feeling tone or emotional climate of our interaction with each other. In other words, early life interactions with important others are stored in the form of representations of the self emotionally interacting with significant others, and these mental representations are cognitive-emotional units that consist of a self-representation, a representation of the other and a linking, mediating feeling. Thus our early inner representations of relationships have a natural emotional energy, an emotional charge, built into them. And in the first year of life, the repeated experience of being an elated baby with a joyful and adoring mother gradually helps us build a picture of ourselves and our mother within this relationship and the positive emotions that suffuse our interactions. Once these portraits have been encoded by our cortico-limbic loops, activating this positive representation or portrait of ourselves becomes a powerful way to evoke the positive emotions that accompanied these early life interactions. Evoking the representation of happy baby with happy mother recreates the emotion of happiness and elation that was taken in along with these earlier interactions. The absorption and coalescence of positive experiences in the outside world eventually form the internal cortical reins that steer the limbic system toward a happier, more joyful state.

The development of our pleasure circuit during the first year of life occurs in an upward spiral of growth that promotes further growth. For example, dopamine stimulates the orbitofrontal cortex to make new connections with the limbic system, which in turn creates the right neurochemical environment for the development of the toddler's growing internal representations of himself and important others. These representations, in turn, allow the child to invoke pleasurable states for himself and to learn to regulate their intensity. Our internal pictures of people, including ourselves, are prime regulators (or dysregulators) of our emotions.

One consequence of the fact that we learn to modulate our emotional states in the setting of our early life relationships with caretakers is that many of our most important feelings are inextricably peopled. In other words, emotional states such as happiness or sadness or anger tend to be accompanied by a simultaneous activation of an inner representation of the self in relationship to another person rooted in our past experience of that emotional state. Thus, our inner emotional states are entangled with our ever-evolving mental image of ourselves and others and our relationship to one another. The portraits of our emotional relationships are stored in the cortex and evoked later as needed to help us regulate our own inner states. The more strongly positive the pictures we form in early life are, the stronger the internalized inner images we have to fall back on in times of distress. Thus, the stronger our cortical reins over our limbic system, the more effective our attempts to tame our inner feelings become.

It is worth noting that these internal pictures do not rely on specific memories from early life of how things were with Mom. We don't sit around thinking about that time Mom figured out we were hungry and fed us. Instead, the part of the brain that can encode explicit memories of particular events ("Mom fed me strained carrots today") is not even "on-line" yet and will not be until about eighteen to twenty-four months. (Hence the fact that we don't remember anything about very early life; for most of us our first explicit memories are from around age two or later.) In contrast, the part of our brain that functions later in life when we learn a skill or a way of doing something, such as how to ride a bicycle or how to serve a tennis ball, is already up and running from birth. What we are actually encoding in these early life experiences is the *process* of our interaction with Mom. The skill we are learning using this alternate type of memory (known as implicit memory) is how to be with another person.[7]

Daniel Stern has called the important early inter-

actions that take place between mother and infant
conveying a process or a way of being or relating to
another person "vitality affects." Though we tend to
think of the various emotions as different ice cream
flavors (say, chocolate fudge brownie for happiness
and bitter lemon sorbet for sadness), Stern's vitality
affects are feeling states with a rhythm to them rather
than a specific flavor. An example would be a "rush,"
the process of crescendoing intensity, whether it be a
rush of adrenaline, the feeling evoked by the sound
of a powerful wave hitting the beach, the sensation of
a horse breaking into a gallop, the surge of happiness
that mother and baby feel on meeting again after a
separation, or the surge of fear we feel as the roller
coaster nears the top of the hill. While vitality affects
convey something important about the shape of our
experience, they often tell us little about the flavor
of feelings that accompany it. A person explosively
bursting into a run and a person explosively bursting
into a room are both explosively bursting. But each
might be feeling a different blend of joy, anger, or
fright. Explosively bursting is a process, a way of doing something. Stern posits that the infant, like an
audience member at a dance performance, observes
the parent and experiences the main vitality affects
with which primary figures in his life go about their

daily routines, including their interactions with him. In other words, it's the way you wear your hat, the way you sip your tea, how you eat the ice cream rather than the flavor of the ice cream itself, to which your baby is truly attending.[8]

In fact, much of early life interactions prior to the development of spoken language is predicated on the sharing of vitality affects, or ways of being, between mother and infant. A mother's ability to participate in the development of the pleasure circuitry in the first year of life depends on this capacity for attunement, for tuning into the rhythm of the baby's interaction and sharing it. And a mother often shows that she is affectively attuned to her child when she imitates the child's predominant vitality affect in another sensory modality. For instance, if a child reacts to a jumping jack popping out of its box, by flapping his hands furiously, an attuned and communicative mother will take up his current way of being—frenetic surprise—and mirror it by raising and lowering her eyebrows while saying "ee-oo-ee-oo!" in rhythm with his flapping. In this way a child knows that mother really understands the experience, its shape and contours, and wants to share it with him. Mirroring the child's way of being in another sensory modality is important because it highlights the process and the rhythm of his experience and lets him know that Mom is not simply mimicking (or worse, mocking) him. We know that infants can understand this sort of mirroring in a different sensory modality because they have an inborn, "hardwired" ability known as cross-modal perception that allows them to "sync up" different sensory modalities. That means a baby who sucks on a bumpy nipple will recognize (and prefer) it later when shown a bumpy and a smooth nipple. Or that a baby shown two silent films while a soundtrack to one of the films plays will watch the film that the soundtrack "matches." In other words, infants can indeed understand that the same pattern in a different sensory modality is the same, from the day they are born.

Examples of vitality affects are ubiquitous in early caretaker–child interactions. In one study Stern and his colleagues videotaped mothers playing with their children as they would at home. The researchers found that vitality affect expressions occurred in the infants at the rate of about one per minute. About half the time, mothers showed an attunement response to these expressions; in other words, the mother was reflecting to the child an understanding of his current way of being about once every two minutes. And when Stern pointed out these examples on a videotape and asked mothers why they reacted in this way, they typically said they were trying to "share the infant's experience." Stern postulates that these early caretaker–child interactions help babies begin to recognize that internal feeling states are important parts of human experience. As he puts it, "What is at stake here is nothing less than the shape of and extent of the shareable inner universe." These early attunement experiences probably set the stage for empathy for others in later life, for understanding that others have inner worlds of emotional experience, too, and that we can join them in those worlds.

Research suggests that a mother must possess this capacity for affective attunement in order to stretch and push the limits of her child's ability to tolerate various feeling states in a way that helps optimism's neural circuitry evolve optimally. Infant researcher Beatrice Beebe and colleagues have studied the emotional tango of parents and infants by analyzing, frame by frame, videotapes of the facial expressions of four-month-old babies and their mothers. To start, the mother joins the baby where he is, perhaps regarding him with the same neutral (neither frowning nor smiling) face with which he is regarding her. The mother might lead, initiating a smile that is like inviting the infant on an exciting adventure, or she might follow the baby's lead as an increasingly big smile emerges, culminating in the joyous, round-mouthed smile we all enjoy seeing in infants. The mother's attunement helps to guarantee that the pair are generally moving in the same direction, rising or falling together on the scale of positive and negative emotions, sharing the shape and rhythm of the experience. This process happens very rapidly, within fractions of a second, suggesting that both partners are continuously processing emotionally laden facial information from the other and responding in kind nearly immediately. In other words, it is not as if the baby waits for a stimulus from the mother and then responds; instead both parties are processing an ongoing stream of stimuli and responding while the stimulation is still occurring. This mutual inter-activity is probably what leads to the experience of emotional attunement and allows the pair to feel connected, on the same wavelength with each other.

Through interactive processes like facial matching, mothers give their babies an emotional jump-start and join them on their affective journey. But the matching is not 100%. In fact, in successful play interactions, mothers and babies match each other's expressions perfectly about 30% of the time and are slightly mismatched the rest of the time. When mismatches occur, the pair generally return to a matched state within several seconds. But it is these brief periods of slight mismatch that probably serve as the beginning of a wedge between mother and baby, starting to stretch the baby to develop his own capacity for self-regulation, as well as creating a growing sense of the separateness of mother and self.[9] In effect, an infant gets a few seconds to experience an emotion on his own, like a child whose father lets go of his bike seat for a few seconds and lets the child balance on his own before latching on again. Because the rifts of mismatch are brief and quickly repaired, the experience also begins to show infants that they can stay in a relationship even in moments of strain and emotional mismatch and that such interpersonal rifts are reparable. Parents are, simply put, our first emotional pacemakers. By training us through thousands of mutual interactions in each and every hour in early life, they literally shape the ways in which we come to modulate our own inner states.

Evidence from infant observers hints at what happens when things go awry in this first stage of positive amplification. When Daniel Stern asked mothers without a history of depression to become "stone-faced," that is, unresponsive to their infants' attempts to engage them in interactions that produce attunement and positive affect, the babies protested and cooed, attempting to reengage their mothers. But as the mothers remained stone-faced for several minutes, the infants quickly gave up, becoming listless and dejected-looking themselves and failing to seek the mutually regulating interactions that they had craved moments before. When Stern then asked normal mothers to deliberately misattune themselves to their babies, such as jiggling the baby's bottom more slowly and out of sync with the baby's cooing or arm-flapping rhythms, the babies looked quizzically over their shoulders at Mom as if to say "What's wrong?" These findings hint at what might happen when a depressed or otherwise impaired mother fails to participate normally in the attunement and positive amplification cycle in the first year of life.

Furthermore, Beebe documented the problematic interaction pattern that can rapidly develop when mothers override their infants' nascent attempts at self-regulation through gaze aversion and insist instead on maintaining a connection through eye contact. This "chase-and-dodge" pattern in which the infant tries to disengage while the mother pursues him and attempts to reengage him might result when a mother's ability to understand her baby's need is impaired or when she cannot tolerate the loss of connection herself. The baby is learning that "as I move away, you move in, and as you move in, I move away." This means much of the baby's energy is being used to manage "being away from" rather than "being with" the mother. These findings suggest that problems in this first phase of the mood-modulation process might begin to create problems for the infant, such as access to a limited range of positive feelings or the expectation that others will be intrusive and overstimulating within relationships.

If attunement is important in stretching an infant's capacity to tolerate increasingly positive feeling states, in the second year of life, all hell breaks loose. There is a major shift in how he is treated by caretakers, with mother no longer simply seeking to assuage all his negative feelings through comforting, stroking, or otherwise modulating the tot. Instead, parents begin to act as if they increasingly expect their child to tolerate and regulate negative feelings for himself. The tenor of caretaker–child interactions changes, with the number of interactions that involve correction increasing sharply. One study even showed that toddlers in the second year of life receive a prohibition from their primary caretaker about every nine minutes.[10] That's a lot of correction—no wonder everybody's cranky during this period! The task of this period is for the child to increasingly develop and expand his capacity to control negative emotions and the impulses to act that accompany them; as in later life, being socially appropriate frequently depends upon quashing the desire to act on or show our negative feelings.

During this period, maternal prohibitions in the form of stern looks, lack of response, or irate words become more frequent. Of course, these responses are not what the child has come to expect amid the experience of attunement in the first year of life. And the experience of being emotionally out of sync with Mom triggers a sense of shock and emotional deflation in the infant. In essence, the caretaker slams on the brakes, sending the child into a shame-filled, negative, low-arousal state that he is not yet capable of regulating for himself. The child who has been thrown into this state looks like a wet dishrag—limp, with little or no body movement, dejected, as if his bubble had been burst. It is as if he has been cruising at sixty, borrowing the mother's positive responses for fuel and gradually learning how to fuel himself. But when she withdraws the supply he still relies on and even reprimands him, he is stopped dead in his tracks, feeling ashamed, alone, and angry simultaneously.

Having used her power to affect the toddler's inner state in a way that shapes his behavior in a socially desirable direction, the caretaker then must re-engage the child and repair the rupture in the relationship caused by her disapproval. This process of repair is just as crucial as the disapproval itself. Without disapproval, the child cannot learn to tolerate—and regulate—the negative feelings that occur in the face of disapproval from others. In turn, he will remain fragile and overly dependent on praise for positive self-esteem, and he will remain selfish, convinced that his wants and needs are more important than the interests and desires of others. Without repair, the toddler is left for a protracted time in a state of deflated negative emotions, including anger, sadness, and shame, and he has yet to develop an effective means to pull himself out of these states. He is left thrashing about in a morass of negative emotion. Just imagine how easy it might be for a depressed or angry caretaker, who struggles with negative emotional states herself, to fail to repair the rift in the relationship. But the repair process is essential because it restores the child's positive feeling state, including his positive feelings about himself, making it clear that while Mom may not love what he did or how he acted, she does love and forgive him. The process also teaches children to endure negative feeling states and to expect to come out on the other end of them with positive feelings and intact relationships with others. Through this process of disapproval and misattunement followed by reconnection and reattunement, early caretakers increasingly teach the child to tolerate and ultimately manage intense negative feelings on his own. This process of disruption and repair gives the child an inner portrait of an angry mother and a bad, angry, or ashamed self to add to his growing cortical photo album for future reference. In addition, when all goes well, it leaves him with a model of relationships in which the self can be forgiven for errors, and the portrait of an angry mother does not obscure the possibility of repair of the relationship with its return to a loving and satisfied mother. This process of rupture and repair increasingly gives the child the ability to modulate negative emotional states for himself.[11]

A second circuit is developing during this period, in an adjacent part of the brain to the first loop. The growth of this new circuit is influenced by the disapproval–repair cycle between child and caretaker characteristic of this period, with neurons in the second circuit that, interestingly enough, actually seem to grow faster and better under the influence of the stress hormone cortisol (released when the child is in a low-arousal state, such as the one seemingly produced by the caretaker's disapproval). That means the rupture-and-repair process may actually be crucial to the development of the neural circuitry through which we increasingly manage negative feelings for ourselves, setting the stage chemically for optimal neuronal growth and development. The caretaker of this period is thus not only exercising the infant's capacity to be more separate and self-regulating, but is also literally sculpting this second set of neuronal connections that the child will use for self-regulation of negative emotional states over time.

As these cortical circuits mature in sequence, the child is all the while forming more and more complex representations of his caretakers and of his interactions with them. These inner images may help him to feel elated, to soothe himself, or to tolerate negative feedback from others without being plunged into despair. These feelings always occur in the context of a relationship to others; emotions evolve and develop and become increasingly refined through the process of our interactions with others. Young children are often seen doing things that suggest they are evoking internal representations for the purposes of mood regulation. For instance, a toddler may sing both parts of a song she frequently shares with mother, to generate positive feelings or to ward off anxiety in the face of separation from mother, evoking her mother's loving presence by recalling a shared positive experience. Similarly, a child may reach out with one hand to swipe a forbidden cookie, then stop herself with the other hand as if the hand of Mom had suddenly come on the scene to stop her. And indeed, the hand of Mom—in the form of an activated inner snapshot of situations past—is indeed increasingly present even when Mom herself is not. What starts as external brain training by early caretakers ultimately results in the etching of inner circuits, based on this training, that endure and shape, even in their absence, our ability to regulate our inner states later in life.

As you may have guessed, the cortico-limbic circuits that develop in early life are also intimately related to self-esteem and its regulation. In fact, self-esteem can be defined as "an affective picture of the self," with high self-esteem connoting a predominance of positive affects about the self, such as pride, and low self-esteem connoting an abundance of negative emotions about the self, such as shame. Effective emotional regulation, which results in a preponderance of positive affects such as enjoyment and excitement, also results in high self-esteem as well as positive pictures of others. In contrast, problematic mood modulation that leads to sadness, anxiety, and anger is usually accompanied by more negative views of the self and others around us. Because our loops for limbic control are forged between our emotional centers and the areas of the cortex responsible for encoding psychological snapshots of ourselves and others, feelings occur in the context of current relationships or are related to the remembrance of relationships past. For better or worse, our inner emotional states are peopled by mothers and others included in the snapshot album in our heads. Although we are born with little ability to influence our limbic systems, we quickly develop inner reins in the form of loops between the cortex and limbic system that are forged in the context of early affective interactions with others to assist us with the task of mood modulation. When all goes well, our cortex can help to control our limbic system, with these inner snapshots of ourselves and others helping us to modulate our moods effectively.

As the second year of life progresses, another important change in emotional self-modulation occurs: the development of spoken language. With the advent of language (which, in contrast to the emotional regulatory circuits discussed earlier, is a largely left hemispheric event), mothers and their children begin progressively to talk more and more about internal states. Verbal discussion of and reflections about emotional experiences can occur, whereas communication prior to language revolved more around the sharing of vitality affects. Beginning around eighteen months, talking about feelings starts with merely commenting on them or labeling them. By twenty-eight months, about 60% of mothers' speeches to their children involve references to internal states. By the time children approach age three, half of the conversations they have about feelings are about the causes of feeling states. This process of speaking about feelings, giving them labels and language, is important because it is through their talk that parents teach children how to recognize what they are feeling, and to what and whom their feelings are connected. In addition, speaking about feelings allows parents to communicate to their children what constitutes acceptable expression of feelings and also to explain techniques for emotional regulation and self-control that children can utilize as they continue to refine their mood-modulatory skills. There is great variability, however, in how much families talk about feelings, with an average of about 8½ conversations per hour (where a conversation is defined as two or more speaker "turns" or comments between a child and someone else) and a range of 2 to 25 conversations per hour. Furthermore, how well these conversations go has implications for later emotional communication skills. The more mothers talked to children at age three about emotions, the more skilled the children were in evaluating emotional reactions in others at age six. Furthermore, the discussion of feelings allows children to construct an ever more complex portrait of others, and this increased understanding translates into increased empathy as well.[12] So it is sad and ironic, though perhaps not unexpected, that when researchers studied a group of maltreated children, they found they had less words for negative emotions such as hatred, anger, and disgust even as they presumably had more experiences with these emotions in themselves and others. This suggests that they had failed to get the opportunity to learn to connect feeling states with words, perhaps setting the stage for a condition called alexithymia (literally "lack of words for feelings") in later life in which people cannot understand and differentiate what they are feeling or comprehend what produces particular kinds of feeling states in themselves and others.[13]

Finally, there is evidence that our capacities for mood modulation do evolve more effectively when we are given real control—and the tools for self-control—in early life. Research has shown that parents who used less coercion, guiding and limiting their children's behaviors by explaining what is expected and why without resorting to threats or force when their children were two, had five year olds with better moods and relationships with others (including parents!) and higher levels of curiosity, exploration, and autonomy.[14] Put differently, parents who did not control their children in a severe, bossy, and mercenary way and did not engage in power struggles but, rather, geared their interventions toward giving the child the inner resources to achieve control by understanding what was expected and why produced children with more positive views of themselves and others, more robustly positive moods, and more independence. Like Seligman's helplessness-immunized dogs, these children presumably had more frequent experiences of actually controlling things in their environment, of having an impact on the world around

them, of finding that their actions made a difference and that their wishes and desires carried weight.
Because they spent less time feeling helpless and
ashamed or angry, they presumably also had more experiences of being in control of themselves as well.

While early life experiences are of crucial importance when it comes to learning to modulate our
own inner states, biological factors such as temperament also play a key role. For example, Kagan's ob-
servation of four hundred four-month-old infants led
him to characterize one third of them as highly reac-
tive, demonstrating that they exhibited greater increases in heart rate and more fear in response to
novel stimuli.[15] Similarly, Davidson's work in infants
demonstrated that he could predict which would
cry when their mothers left the room, based upon
whether their left (associated with an upbeat temperament) or right (associated with a melancholy,
fretful temperament) frontal lobes were more active.[16]
His studies represent an impressive new link between
a particular attitude toward the world and a specific
pattern of brain activation. But what if you are born
with a more active right frontal lobe? Is the ballgame
over before it has begun? No. Temperament is not
destiny. Kagan found that parents who pushed their
timid children could make them bolder during child-

hood, while overprotective parents made their children more fearful. Davidson's research suggests that while it may be impossible to shift our right-to-left frontal lobe balance, certain patterns of positive and negative thought can affect the right and left frontal lobes differentially. Although biological factors such as temperament or predisposition to mood disorders can also play a role in determining how easy or difficult it will be to gain a sense of mastery over our emotions, the nature of the limbic lessons we receive in the context of our early life relationships will determine how our genetic and biological potential is ultimately expressed. The vital limbic lessons of early life determine whether we can competently modulate our own moods and achieve the autonomy and optimistic perspective that effectively regulating our inner feelings can bring.

Chapter Five

THE TIES
THAT BIND

As I hesitantly start to kiss the woman in my dream, our jaws suddenly lock and our chins fuse so that we only have one shared lower face. Somehow I know that one or the other of us will have to bite his way free. One of us will not survive. I am loathe to make the first move, but if I wait for her to strike it may be too late and I'll be destroyed. I sit apprehensive but motionless.

"That's it," you said in my dream as you escorted me to the door. "What do you mean, that's it?" I asked, already feeling anxious and full of dread. "That's it. We're through. We won't be meeting anymore," you answered. "Now that you got your promotion you don't need me." I felt sick.

In my dream, I've taken my girlfriend on a double black diamond trail. I'm standing at the top of the hill watching as she starts to ski down. Part of me is waiting to laugh at her if she looks foolish, sitting down on her butt and sliding down the hill because she can't hack the slope or something. Another part of me wonders if it was stupid to bring her up here and what will I do if she breaks her leg.

FOR EVERY CHILD who emerges from childhood having essentially learned to tame the beasts of anger, anxiety, and sadness, and having been equipped with representations of himself and others in relationships that are infused with positive emotions, there is another, less fortunate child. His early life experiences have left him with cognitive–affective structures in which powerful negative feeling states like shame, anger, guilt, contempt, and loneliness play a central role. As mentioned in the last chapter, we take in the relationship experiences of early life in what Otto Kernberg has termed "self–object–affect" units.[1] In other words, each relationship representation encodes one picture of our self and one of the other person (or "object" in psychoanalytic terms) as well as the emotional or affective coloration of a given interpersonal interaction. These early life interactions are literally a part of the brain structure, encoded as they are in the cortico-limbic loops, where our growing cortical portraits of self and other are strongly linked to particular limbically generated emotions. This growing cognitive–affective structure, established in early life, is evoked later as a model of how to be with another person and what to expect in relationships, thereby shaping and guiding all later life interactions with others. In fact, when Lester Luborsky and his colleagues at the University of Pennsylvania asked people to tell ten stories—real or imagined, from the past or the present—they found that each individual's stories reflected a typical plot line, revealing their inner portrait of how people relate and what emotions characterize their interactions. Their research suggests that the cognitive–affective, cortico-limbic connections forged in early life persist into adulthood and shape in an enduring way the way we relate to others. The core emotional themes around which our relationships revolve can even be seen clearly in the stories of our dreams, including the dreams of three of my patients, which opened this chapter.[2]

Michael's dream, which begins with a kiss and ends in an anxious deadlock, reveals his characteristic mode of relating. One of his options in relationships is to remain disconnected and distant, to avoid the kiss altogether. Another is to engage in interactions with others that begin with the pleasant promise of intimacy but devolve into a seemingly life-threatening situation that makes him anxious and apprehensive instead. He can bite his way free first and endure the guilt of having been the attacker. Or he can wait for his partner to bite first and wind up mortally wounded and perhaps angry at being victimized as well. Either way, closeness prefigures destruction; no wonder something that should be pleasant—a kiss that symbolizes an intimate relationship, a bond—is instead something that Michael is hesitant about. Notice how every possible relationship permutation is pervaded by negative emotional possibilities—the loneliness of remaining disconnected and distant, the merger and loss of the whole self that comes with being close, the guilt of "saving face" by attacking first, the anxiety produced by waiting with the expectation of being attacked, the anger that accompanies such an attack. Who could be optimistic while struggling with such attitude and feelings?

As a brief aside, notice that Freudian psychology might lead us to focus more on the sexuality in the dream, the kiss itself. But because a person's sexuality occurs in the setting of relationships, it is itself colored by the relational patterns laid down in early life. Thus, in Michael's case there was also a link between the closeness of sexuality and the threat of destructive aggression. For instance, he worried about women "giving in" to their own sexual pleasure and paying for the enjoyment of intercourse with an unwanted pregnancy, a child that might burden them forever. The closeness that intercourse offered was anxiety provoking because it also contained a destructive threat, a price to be paid for the intimacy. I have found that the understanding of early life relationship representations is a necessary precursor to unraveling the mysteries of a patient's sexual inhibitions and fantasies.

Jill's dream reveals a different but also problematic perspective on the emotional climate of interpersonal relationships. She dreams that I, her therapist of more than three years, precipitously, unilaterally, and without warning decide to terminate our relationship without further discussion, simply announcing as she leaves a session that we are finished. When I explored with her what her recent promotion would have to do with my decision not to see her anymore, she focused on themes of guilt and responsibility, betrayal and retribution. If she moved on she saw herself damaging our connection in some crucial way, and she would feel guilty about that. If leaving me behind was her crime, my decision to stop seeing her was the punishment for her betrayal. Furthermore, rather than giving her fair warning and letting her know I was hurt or displeased or felt abandoned, I would simply store up my feelings of being angry and betrayed until our connection to one another was irreparably damaged. And though I might feel upset, what would show on the surface was a kind of icy, steely coolness, a capacity to cut her out of my life without feeling it. Jill has taken in a model of how relationships operate in which the cost of independence and autonomy is a sense of guilt and of having betrayed someone else, in which moving on or moving away might well mean losing the relationship forever. She has the capacity to feel warmly connected in relationships, to experience positive emotions. But hers is still a model in which certain relationship ruptures are irreparable, and this fact infuses all her relationships with the anxiety that she might trigger such a catastrophic event without even realizing that the other person is reaching the limits of their tolerance. Because both staying and going were suffused with negative feeling, Jill found it impossible to feel optimistic about herself and the world around her for long.

In Robert's dream, he places his girlfriend in a situation that she may or may not be able to handle and then watches in a distant, aloof manner to see what will happen. He is poised to laugh contemptuously if she shows a lack of control and skill and slides down the ski slope on her derrière, but he also has some anxiety about the idea that she might really crash and burn, breaking her leg in the process. And there's the unavoidable fact that his turn to go down the expert slope is fast approaching as well, with the unasked— and as yet unanswered—question of how *he'll* do when put to the test. Robert's relationships are often pervaded by this type of unemotional dissection of the stuff of which others are made, and he often attempts to put them in situations where he might get to see them "lose it." To the extent that they don't, he idealizes and reveres their self-control, but when they do show emotion or other signs that they are affected by a situation or by others, he is bothered by their weakness. But his desire to know whether and how they will lose control comes at a price—he has to worry about his role in having put them in a situation in which they might get hurt, his role as an aggressor, and he has to wonder whether the tables might not be turned in an instant, whether his girlfriend won't soon be waiting at the bottom of the ski slope, watching him, ready to be contemptuous of him if he should falter. In fact, he is constantly worrying about what is showing about himself and how good his capacity for self-control really is as he seeks to hide the fact that others do indeed have an impact on him. This constant testing of himself and others and his sense that relationships revolve around emotionally unhinging others means that Robert cannot sustain an optimistic stance toward himself and others.

The stories each of these patients tells from early life dovetail with the images about how relationships work contained in their dreams. Raised by his stepmother after his mother's death, Michael remembered that often when his stepmother was angry she would criticize him for something until he cried and then both tease him for crying and tell him to stop. If he wouldn't stop she might force him to go and select the branch from a tree in the backyard with which he would "prefer" to be whipped for his failure to do as she said. While her wrath was often without rhyme or reason, one thing that seemed to predictably provoke it was any "show-off" behavior on his part, even actions that sounded like the typical "look at me" pride of a child enjoying his accomplishments. His stepmother seemed to interpret this behavior as cocky or grandiose rather than praising his accomplishments; she also demanded that each and every one of her actions, such as making dinner for the family, be praised. Yet despite these unpleasant interactions, as in his dream, Michael chose to hesitantly engage his stepmother. Simply withdrawing was not an option because, as he poignantly put it, "she was the only mother I had." So trying to be close and enduring the anxiety her potential to turn on him generated as well as the anger her attacks stirred within him was the only course. Furthermore, in keeping with the merger and loss of individuality hinted at through the fusion of chins in the dream, his grandmother would often finish sentences for him, creating the illusion of being so close that she and Michael were thinking and feeling simultaneously on the one hand and yet setting a new standard for intrusiveness and control on the other.

The emotional tendencies and relationship expectations Michael forged in his relationship with his stepmother did indeed linger into adulthood. For instance, upon finding himself in a confrontational situation at work, Michael would often find that the more furious he became, the more tongue-tied and motionless he became as well. While he becomes anxious about his abilities and highly self-critical in the face of any perceived attack on his work, he is equally anxious about his abilities when things are going well, and he is enjoying himself and feeling capable. He feels that all it would take for a fatal attack to occur would be one misstep that would wipe out all the things he has done right on the job. And the feeling that he is often sitting perfectly still on a hotbed of angry feelings in order to contain them also means that there is always the possibility that he could himself finally explode as well. In later life Michael often took the pathway of remaining disconnected and apart from others rather than risking the angry and dangerous struggles he envisioned. But this stance came with quite a high emotional cost, with Michael complaining that he felt "grayed" out, lacking in spontaneity and disconnected from everything and everyone. In other words, nothing affected him too negatively, but nothing was too much fun, either.

If the early life relationship model that Michael has encoded centers around either standing apart and enduring a kind of bland aloneness or becoming close to the point of merging, then enduring the risk that the closeness will end in a bloodbath, Jill's way of relating might be characterized by moving away from another person, feeling guilt and responsibility for leaving them behind, then retreating, moving closer to them again but feeling angry about the independence and forward motion she has given up. Jill's mother, depressed and bedridden for much of Jill's childhood due to medical illness, was both a colorful and compelling character, but Jill had the constant (and realistic) fear of her mother dying, disappearing on her. Jill proved to be an entertainer with the will, warmth, and skills to rescue her mother from her dark moments of despair, seeming at times to serve almost as a kind of human antidepressant agent. But what happens when someone abruptly ceases taking an antidepressant? Withdrawal. The problem with such an early life relationship with her mother for Jill was to put a high price on Jill's independence. Her desire to be separate and do her own thing seemed to threaten her mother's very health and well-being as effectively as if she had suddenly stopped a much needed drug. Since her mother was not only depressed and at times needy but also someone Jill loved and adored, the temptation to tie herself to her mother and never leave was overwhelming, as was the guilt when Jill thought about being more separate and venturing out into the world to do things that interested her. To further complicate matters, Jill's depressed mother was probably not entirely grateful; she was probably also furious with herself for being needy, depending on her daughter to bolster her moods, and felt guilty for holding her daughter back. And she was probably secretly angry with Jim for having so much impact on how she felt. When the two would fight, her mother would sometimes angrily remind Jill that sometimes people "snapped," did things that were so terrible that they could not be forgiven. This threat of withdrawal of her mother's love was a fight ender; who could press for their independence if it meant giving up such a special and important tie? Jill would retreat to avoid having her attachment to her mother broken like a rubber band stretched too far. But considering all of her sacrifices for her mother, Jill could not help being angry when her mother threatened to withdraw her love. When her mother sensed Jill's desire to attack her, she fell back on her illness as a way to avoid responsibility, claiming that Jill was "killing" her with her anger. But after such devotion on Jill's part over all that time, how could her mother not then feel angry at herself for attacking her essentially loyal daughter. And round and round the spiral of loyalty and betrayal, anger and guilt, would go.

Jill's propensity in later life was to choose men who struggled with problematic feeling states like depression that she had to help them buffer and who were extremely sensitive to any hint that Jill might be moving away from them and into her own independent endeavors. Like her mother, the men were also angry with her because they secretly relied on her and indeed often threatened to unilaterally end their relationships. In response to the repeated enactment of this relationship pattern, Jill frequently felt tempted to throw off all attachments and go it alone, to steel herself to be strong and independent without anyone else in the picture. But her fears of her own loneliness and depressed mood, and her inability to regulate her inner states effectively for herself kept her attached, albeit in a problematic way, to others.

In contrast to Jill, Robert's early life experiences with his mother could be characterized as competitions to see who could be the most emotionally indifferent and unaffected, who had the most self-control under duress, who would "lose it," and with what provocation. When he was a boy, Robert's mother repeatedly let him pack his belongings and run away from home without so much as a good-bye or an "I'll miss you," often showing him to the front door herself and inviting him to go. While Robert put up a good show of being happy to leave home by day, sometimes when he ran away he would find himself several blocks from home as darkness fell, hungry, tired, and lonely, and no longer able to feign indifference. He would find himself crying out of loneliness and frustration, drying his eyes before he returned home in a humiliated state to a mother who refused to admit she was glad—or even relieved—to see him. At other times, when he was gone for too long, his mother would "lose it" herself, becoming frantic and searching for him in the car until she found him, then crying and screaming at him while she drove him home. On these occasions, Robert would torture her by continuing to try to get away, threatening to jump from the moving vehicle, taking her increased anger and upset in response to these threats as a sign that she did in fact care. Part of what he soon learned from her was how to turn the tables on other people, provoking them, then watching in contemptuous fascination as they struggled to mask their upset while he calmly, coolly didn't bat so much as an eye. In reality, Robert was secretly incredibly affected by others and would often go to great lengths to please them and to be sure that they were beholden to him but not the reverse. In the psychotherapeutic relationship with me, he prized my ability to mask my reactions to what he said and did, whether it was controlling my laughter at his humorous remarks or masking my feelings if he criticized something I wore or a new haircut. He was both fascinated to see whether I felt anything behind my seemingly collected veneer and terrified that if I were to reveal my true reactions to things—or even the fact that I had reactions—I would lose his respect and be effectively worthless in his eyes. Another consequence of all this masking of emotion was that Robert could never trust that he was getting the real story, the whole truth, from what people said or how they reacted. Only if he could actually get inside their brains and see what they were thinking would he really know who they were and what they thought of him.

Interestingly, each of my patients also had dreams during the course of treatment that seemed to revolve around themes of emotional control. For instance, on one occasion Michael dreamed that he took his car to a mechanic because when the accelerator was pressed, nothing happened. After a careful examination the mechanic assured him that all the parts were there and in proper operating condition but that there was a wire loose, a severed connection, so that even when Michael pushed the gas pedal down as hard as he could, nothing would happen. The mechanic also assured Michael that the problem was not so serious that it couldn't be fixed. Michael related the dream's imagery to the lack of control he could exert over both his negative and his positive feelings. If the car was a self-portrait, he reasoned, then the dream was saying that even when he revved himself up, the car wouldn't accelerate because of this loose connection. So he ended up with lots of wishes and fantasies that he couldn't turn into action. It was safe to stoke these daydreams as long as he never shifted out of neutral, because although neutral left him feeling mired and ineffectual in the world around him, it was the only gear in which he could be sure that his feelings, especially anger, were safely regulated. After all, if you can't be sure the car won't suddenly accelerate to seventy and that you won't have a disastrous crash, perhaps you're better off leaving it in neutral. But the cost is that you also cannot throw yourself into the excited, joyous, and exuberant high gear that makes life colorful. No wonder Michael complained that he spent much of his time feeling "grayed out" and bland.

My patients' stories of adulthood relationships in work, love, and play, and the patterns that emerged in their relationships with me were intricately entwined with both their ability to modulate their own moods and their capacity for various emotional states. But although each had specific issues to grapple with, none of the three could rein in and regulate his own negative and beastly feelings effectively. Because negative feelings like shame, anger, and anxiety colored their perspectives, none of the three could sustain an optimistic stance either.

In the first two years of life, our circuitry for emotional regulation evolves through maternal attunement and amplification of the positive, followed by the rupture–repair cycle, and later the ability to talk about feeling states and the motivations for them. Problematic early life relationship patterns and the warping of our interpersonal landscapes can skew our emotional palettes and result in difficulty in masterfully managing the emotional states that color our inner lives.

If you were paying careful attention, you noticed that I emphasized that the stories patients tell about their early lives were similar to those stories of their adulthood relationships, rather than asserting that the way their early lives actually *were* accounted for these relationship patterns. It is next to impossible to prove the historical veracity of our early life memories, especially regarding the subtle attitudes and actions of others. In fact, there's been a long debate in psychological circles about whether real early traumatic historical events engender later life pathology or whether the action of a person's own internal drives and fantasies color and distort the way others are seen and internalized from the very beginning of life. Self psychologists, who are proponents of the first approach, believe that the real empathic failures of early caretakers lead to emotions such as anger, and the negative views of self and other that accompany it, as a kind of "toxic" result of these failures. Freudian proponents of other models assert that drives such as aggression naturally color all relationships. But it is easy to put these two models together and to think that empathic failures in early life, such as a failure to mend a relationship rupture, might induce ashamed or angry states in a child that would then—in keeping with the mood-congruent effects discussed in chapter 2—color his thoughts and fantasies about the other person as well as himself. Furthermore, the representations of ourselves and others internalized in early life are probably a combination of real-life experiences elaborated upon by our own fantasies and feeling states. Then these budding relationship models probably become the lens through which our perceptions of future interactions are filtered, in much the same way that our perceptions of the world around us are colored by our present emotional state. In other words, our internalizations about

self and other become not only a record of past relationship interactions combined with the fantasies that
acted upon these real interactions but a shaper of our
future relationships as well, acting as they do to give
us information about what to expect from others.[3]

Given the interplay between reality and fantasy,
past pattern and present perception, which shape our
representations of self and others and the emotions
that tie this interaction together, it is important to
recognize that we cannot make a direct, one-to-one
correspondence between a particular past event and a
specific type of psychopathology. In other words, I
cannot prove that a childhood failure to amplify positive feelings accounts for Michael's joylessness in the
present—too many other variables come into play
over the course of development. For example, a depressed mother might not amplify her infant's positive feelings, but if he is listless and lacks the capacity
for joy and elation in later life, is it a result of this
failure or merely a reflection of his inheritance of her
depressive tendencies? In addition, we've seen that
the cortico-limbic loops, our primary circuitry for
the regulation of both emotions and self-esteem,
evolve during the first two years of life, before both
the advent of spoken language and the capacity
to record memories of specific events. So we have

neither words for nor explicit memories of the repeated interactions that led us to regulate emotions and relate to others in a given way.

Although it is methodologically difficult—if not impossible—to show that specific early life interactions cause particular later life consequences, we do know that the strategies we use to relate to others and to regulate our emotional states in the context of relationships coalesced during the first two years of life. For instance, some adults seem to have simply shut down the expression of all of their feelings, positive and negative alike. They rarely feel especially angry but are never particularly joyful either. Often behind their seemingly aloof and emotionally distant veneers lurks the sense that they are always on the verge of being overwhelmed, that if they allow themselves to feel anything it will be the crack in an otherwise sturdy dam that triggers a torrent of feelings they cannot control, feelings that will make the carefully built dam collapse. This style of emotional management is evident by age two in toddlers who are said to be avoidantly attached to their caretakers. When separated from their mothers, these toddlers are inhibited about displaying feelings of distress and rarely protest or cry. Upon reunion, they do not seem to seek comfort from their mothers nor appear especially happy to see them. Rather, they tend to ignore their mothers altogether when they reenter the room, focusing their attention elsewhere as if they were indifferent. This avoidant attachment style represents a particular kind of strategy for emotional regulation in which the toddler, probably in response to a parent who is intolerant of the expression of both positive and negative feelings, essentially learns to act as if the presence and absence of important others have little or no effect on him.[4] However, elevated levels of the stress hormone cortisol belie the fact that the toddler is actually experiencing high levels of stress or anger that are taking their psychological toll on him.[5] In adulthood, people who have evolved this style of managing emotions most often seem frozen, distant, and unwilling to be affected. In short, they seem to have learned to overregulate emotions so effectively that they often appear to have none. If you recall the extent to which optimism is encouraged by the presence of intensely positive feelings, you can imagine the toll that this emotional distancing and stunting of positive feelings has on their capacity for optimism in adult life. Notice that the patterns that Michael and Robert have evolved for relating to other people contain elements of this avoidant attachment style.

A second common attachment style or strategy of

emotional modulation is known as a resistant or ambivalent attachment style. Toddlers with this style noisily express negative feelings, showing exaggerated signs of distress when their caretaker leaves the room and angry protest when the caretaker returns combined with clingy behavior that reveals their simultaneous desire for soothing and comfort. This simultaneous desire for comfort combined with angry and vocal protest seems to have evolved in the setting of early life relationships in which parents only intermittently responded to their emotional expressions and attended more to the toddler's negative feelings than his positive ones. In adulthood these children often seem dramatic and excessively emotional, maintaining their clingy but angry styles in a manner that seems to say "I hate you. You're abandoning me and inadequate to my needs, but please, please, don't leave me." Their difficulties can be seen more in terms of emotional underregulation, as an inability to adequately inhibit emotions and their expression. Jill's typical mode of relating to others contains elements of this ambivalent attachment style.

In contrast to these avoidant and ambivalent attachment styles, children who have had caretakers who served as good enough emotional teachers evolve a secure attachment pattern in which they can openly display but not excessively exaggerate their feelings of distress and need for comfort, can be effectively soothed, and show a limited amount of anger and stress in their interactions with caretakers. In other words, they neither overregulate their emotional states as avoidantly attached children do nor underregulate them as ambivalently attached children do.

In addition to knowing that the interactions of early life coalesce into a distinctive attachment style during the first two years, research has also shown when subjects were reevaluated at age twenty that there is substantial stability in attachment style at age one, with about two-thirds of securely and avoidantly attached children maintaining their characteristic style into adulthood, whereas only about half of ambivalently attached children maintained that style (presumably because they had somehow learned to regulate their underregulated clingy–angry emotional displays in the interim).[6] In adulthood, those who had been avoidantly attached children tended to be dismissive of emotional interactions. They gave very distanced accounts of their childhoods, with an inability to recall much that was specific about them and with very little present-day emotion. Adults who had been ambivalently attached, in contrast, still seemed preoccupied and overwhelmed by memories of their often traumatic childhoods. In other words, even in adulthood the tendency to overregulate emotions to the point of having none or to underregulate them to the point of continuing to be overwhelmed by feelings from the past was still evident. So, too, was the effective regulation of emotion and self-esteem seen in adults who had been securely attached in child-hood. Termed *autonomous,* these adults were able to give coherent and balanced accounts of their childhoods and to describe and experience a range of positive and negative feelings about their early lives.[7]

Furthermore, evidence suggests that these attachment styles are frequently handed down from parent to child. When expectant mothers were interviewed about the nature of their attachments to their own caretakers and then their infants were studied at one year of age, the mother's attachment style to her own mother described prior to her baby's birth actually predicted her infant's eventual attachment style.[8] It is important to note, of course, that all of this inter-generational transmission may not be completely developmentally driven but may represent an interplay of genetics and early life experience. Arguing against the idea that it is purely genetic, however, is the fact that changes in environmental factors have been clearly shown to change attachment style.[9]

It hardly seems surprising, though, if the purpose of early life is to school the emotions, that the lessons we learn are the lessons our teachers have to teach us. Indeed studies have shown that mothers of babies who become avoidantly attached are unresponsive to emotions in general and are least responsive to their baby's negative feelings. Thus they tend, in effect, to prohibit negative feelings and not to encourage positive ones, contributing to a generalized diminution of the expression of all feelings. In contrast, mothers of ambivalently attached infants are the most responsive to negative emotions but respond inconsistently to all emotional displays. This pattern of maternal response seems to encourage the dramatic, noisy, and under-regulated display of emotions that continues into adulthood. Mothers of secure babies were found to respond to a wider range of both positive and negative emotions in their babies than mothers of insecurely attached infants, in the process teaching their children to experience and tolerate a wider range of all types of emotions for themselves.[10] In pointing out this differential pattern of response, I am not suggesting that you blame your mother for not being the teacher you wish she had been; after all, the lessons she learned presumably depended on the teachers she had as well.

Despite their different patterns of emotional engagement with others, rooted in their unique childhood histories, Michael, Jill, and Robert have one crucial feature in common. They have not internalized a system of mood modulation that enables them to graduate from the emotional schooling in which early life with Mom immerses us. They remain pathologically tied to past patterns. Rather than the smooth evolution from "parent as external emotional guide" to "self as effective internal mood manager" that occurs when all goes well in early life, they are stuck in a mode in which problematic portraits of self and other, and the negative emotional states these internalized pictures evoke, overwhelm their abilities to modulate their own moods.

The ties of early life are indeed ties that bind. They bind particular views of self and other to specific emotional states, literally linking together our emotions and our way of relating to others. The way these pictures of relationships and emotions are tied together will determine if we become autonomous adults who can regulate our own emotions and self-esteem. As we shall see in chapter 6, the alternative is that in adulthood we will continue to rely on others to help us regulate our own inner states and our sense of self-esteem. In remaining bound to others for self-regulation in adulthood, we not only sacrifice self-control, we are also faced with the impossible—and frustrating—task of attempting to control them in order to sustain a comfortable inner state. If good enough caretaking leaves us with an inner island of self-control that sets the stage for autonomy in later life, less-good parenting can in effect leave us with peninsulas instead, with land bridges that connect us to others in problematic ways. In the next chapter, I'll give you an up-close look at the moment-to-moment emotional fluctuations of my patient Isabel during a psychotherapy session. I'll show you the high price of having to extract certain reactions from others—having to arrange and align our interactions with them in the real world so that they compensate for the shortcomings in our self-regulation systems. We are left not only seeing the glass as half empty, but feeling ourselves to be half empty as well.

Chapter Six

THE HALF-EMPTY SELF

I dreamed that I was at the store looking for a special kind of Danish hair conditioner that was made with beer. I knew it was an extravagance, an unnecessary expense, but I just felt I had to have it. My hair is my best feature. I could picture the bottle—glossy label, elegantly shaped—but I knew that the conditioner was even more of a rip-off than it seemed because the bottle was already half empty when you bought it. But that didn't matter to me. I felt desperate to get it, unwilling to compromise. The clerk said the store didn't carry that brand and that she couldn't sell me beer without an ID, but she offered me a kind of hair conditioner that I could mix myself. I knew she was right that I should be able to do it for myself, but I woke up feeling disappointed and upset anyway.

"I GUESS MY FIRST thought about the dream," my patient Isabel began, "is that in it my hair is my best feature. And it's true. It's the only part of me that I really like—that's just the way it should be. That strikes me as a depressing perspective on myself because of course my hair has little to do with who I am inside. In the dream I feel that nice hair is something I'd give just about anything to get. Give me a half-empty bottle. Rip me off. Just let me have what I need. But I have to admit I was a little horrified when I woke up and realized I'd been dreaming about buying beer. Would I really consider risking my sobriety just for nice hair?"

As I listen to Isabel, I find myself worrying a bit. What is this magical Danish elixir, this hair conditioner so special that it could make this beautiful woman—a talented artist who has struggled hard to achieve three years of sobriety—so desperate? After her two years of twice weekly therapy, I also find myself grousing a bit at the idea that her hair is her best feature. It is as if she is criticizing someone I know and like, only that someone is herself. I feel tempted to defend her against her own attack, but I restrain myself for the moment.

As I fret, she continues: "The other thing that stands out about the dream is the bottle being half empty. It's a sign that I'm being extravagant, and probably foolish, buying something that is supposedly refined, European, but really turns out to be already partly used up. Or perhaps never filled up properly in the first place."

I see a familiar picture of Isabel herself beginning to emerge from the dream image of the half-empty bottle of hair conditioner. "It sounds to me like this is another version of the view of yourself we've been talking about. Your packaging is slick, sleek, European. You have glossy, well-conditioned hair, but underneath it you feel secretly like a rip-off, like someone with nothing of real value to offer others. What people see on the surface is not really what you are underneath. The half-empty conditioner bottle is a picture of you."

As a psychiatrist I would usually feel sympathy for a tearful patient. But as Isabel begins to cry silently, large tears rolling down her cheeks, I feel a nagging sense of annoyance instead. I feel puzzled. I muse about what the tears mean in the context of our relationship. Are they a sign that I'm on the mark in speaking of the conditioner as a symbol of Isabel herself? Are they a signal of some kind to me? I find myself wondering if I'm annoyed because Isabel wants me, like everyone else around her, to reassure her that this half-empty view of herself is not really accurate. Perhaps they are not sad tears but angry and demanding ones. I feel manipulated, as if she's exerting a pressure on me to tell her that I see her differently. And it's tempting to tell her so, because, in fact, I do. But I hold my tongue, because I believe that the goal of the type of intensive psychotherapy that we are engaged in is to highlight the rules for relating to others that Isabel's cortico-limbic loops currently contain. Keeping silent may ultimately help to highlight the subtle but controlling psychological maneuvers that Isabel uses in an attempt to get other people to make her feel the way she would like to feel inside—a way that she cannot make herself feel on her own. The good news is that Isabel is not really half empty, even though she feels that way right now, but the bad news is that she may not like what she is full of.

"I guess I'm hopelessly pessimistic," Isabel exclaims finally, with a shrug. "You're right—*I* feel half empty. Maybe it's a view of myself that I can never change. That *we* can never change."

When all goes well in the early life relationship encounters that shape the structure of our cortico-limbic loops, we are left with an inner island of control, an effective, autonomous ability to regulate our own inner states that no longer depends heavily on other people and our interactions with them. In turn, this capacity for mood modulation colors our view of our self. If we spend more time in positive or, at least, comfortable states, then our inner picture of our self will be colored by emotions such as happiness and contentment. But if we spend much of our time in negative inner states such as anxiety or anger, these states will color our sense of self-esteem as well. In effect, self-esteem is an affective portrait of the self, a representation of the self colored by our predominant mood hues. Thus, when certain kinds of parental responses in early life leave us floundering in unregulated, unpleasant emotional states, a secondary consequence is low self-esteem—an affective picture of the self in which our self-concept is tinged with negative emotions. When this happens we end up relying on others to help us regulate both our negative inner states and our sense of self. Although it is normal and acceptable to be dependent on mothers to modulate our moods in early life, it is problematic to remain reliant on others to regulate our inner states in adulthood. What makes it problematic is that our self-esteem now depends on the feedback of others, on eliciting particular reactions from them in order to feel good about ourselves. Of course, because controlling others is ultimately beyond our ability, this method of bolstering and sustaining self-esteem is unlikely to be effective over the long term. Rather than making the shift to an internalized system for regulation of moods and self-esteem, we end up having to try to exert control over others in an attempt to get the goods (and good feelings) needed to sustain ourselves. The subtle maneuvers through which this happens can be seen and understood in psychotherapy by putting our interactions with others, especially our therapist, under the microscope. The therapeutic relationship serves as a kind of laboratory in which we can come to understand the legacy of the style of relating and emotional management that we have learned. In psychotherapy we can learn to observe the shifts in representation of self and other and the emotions that accompany them.

My atypical sense of irritation with Isabel's tears in this particular session serves as a clue to me that she is trying to exert a pull on me, attempting to get me to act in a given way. But rather than just giving in and playing the role in which I have been cast, my job as a psychodynamic psychotherapist is to help her understand why she needs each of us to play certain roles in order for her to feel comfortable inside. Why might she need me to reassure her, for instance, that her hair is not her best feature or that her self is really not half empty, despite the portrait in the dream? And why can't she provide these reassurances herself?

As I ponder these questions, Isabel sits like a forlorn lump in the chair, apparently waiting for my response. In reviewing the interaction thus far, I realize that after I failed to reassure her that her hair is not her best feature, Isabel ups the ante. She sits stonily and silently after I suggest she is half empty, perhaps staging a kind of momentary "strike" against participating in the work that we are trying to do together. Finally, she concurs with my assessment regarding a potential meaning of her dream. But rather than using my remarks to open up a channel of exploration about how she relates to others or what she needs from them, she uses the comment to shut things down. When she asserts that she is hopelessly pessimistic and that nothing we can do together can change her, she in effect retaliates, for my failure to tell her what she wants to hear, by picking up her marbles and going home. I responded empathically to her first comment about her hair even though I ultimately decided not to intervene to counter her attack on herself. But her silence and then her second comment about being half empty and an immutable pessimist irritate me instead. As I reflect upon why, I realize that the problem is that this represents another, more insistent "invitation" from Isabel for me to reassure her, perhaps by injecting an interested energy back into the session and erasing her hopelessness with a cheerful and optimistic remark about her transformation through psychotherapy. Even her tears seem designed to elicit such a response. But because Isabel is seemingly attempting to elicit her desired response, I feel subtly manipulated and controlled and then angry. If I were a friend or lover instead of a therapist (or if I were a therapist who didn't yet understand what was happening between us, as I may well have been in the earlier parts of my therapy with Isabel), I might retaliate myself in response to these feelings of being controlled, perhaps by concurring or ending our discussion. But as a therapist my job is to attempt to understand the minute details of the interaction, not to simply act my part.

After a long and uncomfortable silence, Isabel says, "You must be sick of me. You must feel like kicking me out," before lapsing once again into a sullen sulk. Given that Isabel herself has raised the question of my kicking her out, I decide that my sense of being controlled and the irritation that accompanies it may be correct and that Isabel's comment about being an unchanging pessimist may indeed have been a retaliatory attempt on her part given my lack of response to the script she is expecting us to enact. So I decide to use my own feelings— of irritation and recognition that Isabel is pressuring me for a particular response—to get things moving again.

"I think you'd like for me to tell you that I view you differently," I say. "I wonder if your tears are in part a signal to me that I should say you're not really half empty. Maybe you want me to reassure you that you're beautiful inside and out. But when I fail to do so, you dismiss yourself as a pessimist, unable to change, and anticipate that I am angry with you and discouraged, anxious to be done with you, to angrily kick you out. I think the problem is not that you're hopelessly pessimistic or that you can't change but rather that you cannot depend on your own inner abilities to control how you feel, that you get into these states where you feel down on yourself, then need me or someone else around you to help you get out of them. You're forced to extract the reassurances you need to sustain an inner sense of yourself as good and lovable from us, perspectives that will in turn eradicate your miserable and depressed mood. But your quandary is that you can't possibly feel good and lovable for long when you're secretly, constantly, subtly manipulating others into filling you up with compliments. Sure, it works temporarily for me to re-assure you, but ultimately your need to control other people and pull reassurances out of them makes you feel bad about yourself, and this bad feeling erodes and destroys their reassurances and compliments, leaving you feeling half empty—and in turn in need of extracting compliments from others—once again." I pause to see what Isabel will do with my remarks. I notice that today I'm doing more than my fair share of the talking.

Isabel responds by re-engaging in the task at hand: "I was wondering about the mixture of condi-tioner and beer in the dream on the way to my ap-pointment with you and I thought that maybe what the conditioner does for my hair is what the beer used to do for my moods. I mean, the conditioner makes my hair sleek and glossy. And beer used to make my sense of myself more resilient, my emo-tional life more even. I'd have less anxiety and self-doubt when I was drunk. The alcohol was like a lubricant that prevented me from grinding my inner gears against each other, like motor oil for my emotions. It used to be the only way I knew to try to control how I felt. Or at least to completely eradicate all feeling if it was too overwhelming for me to control. And I suppose it was giving up drinking that landed me in your office in the first place. Because without it I feel raw inside all the time. Then there's the fact, like in the dream, that I seem to have no ID, no identity."

The fact that Isabel re-engages in exploring the dream, and the hints about her ways of relating to others and regulating her emotions that it contains, suggests to me that my comment was not only on the mark but also that it helped to propel us past a momentary deadlock in our interaction with each other. In addition, it seems to have taken us out of the realm of action and interaction and put us into the mind-set of collaboratively exploring and analyzing both the dream and our interactions with each other. This oscillation between the stance of experiencing someone's key relationship patterns as they come to life in therapy and observing the process of relating as it unfolds is the yin and yang through which psychotherapy helps people understand what happens inside them from moment to moment. Enacting with a therapist the process of relating that we learned in early life enables us to see what rules we have encoded about how relationships work. But you may recall that these original interpersonal interactions are neither remembered explicitly nor automatically accessible to language, which happens later. Instead the rules for the process of being with someone are stored in the kind of memory we use for other kinds of processes, like serving a tennis ball or riding a bike. That's why a therapist serves as both an object to re-experience our relationship—a participant—and an observer, a kind of emotional coach who helps us break down and understand what happened in the interaction, what went wrong and how to do it better.

When Isabel thinks about the sense of rawness she often experiences without alcohol, she begins to cry, and this time I feel a sense of genuine empathy with her plight. After all, she did use beer as a kind of internal mood conditioner for years. And now she has given it up, but there's nothing yet to replace it. So her inner state feels tangled and snarled. "What about the clerk in the dream, who tells you she doesn't have what you need and advises you to make it for yourself?" I find myself saying without having made a conscious decision about whether or not to say anything and why. "I thought that was you," Isabel says with a chuckle, rebounding from her tears. "You won't sell me what I want, you want me to make it for myself and that disappoints me." As I see Isabel's mood lift I realize that I have inadvertently and unwittingly helped her to re-regulate her mood and her related sense of self. I have helped to pop her out of a painful inner state and into a more comfortable one with a predictable question to which I am sure she knows the answer. It's comfortable to both of us to explore the possibility that the clerk in the dream is me even if it also amounts to a *New Yorker* cartoon parody of Freud. But then I realize that in the dream, as the clerk, I seem to be stressing the importance of Isabel's emotional independence, insisting that there's a conditioner that she can make for herself, whereas in reality here I am, mixing away in an attempt to give her what she needs to feel better, to get rid of those inner snarls. In response to Isabel's sadness and distress I have stepped back into the process of relating to her in a way that will help her regulate her own inner states, ameliorating her sadness with an upbeat exchange that restores warm and familiar feelings between us and improves her momentary sense of self in the bargain.

Luckily, when I return to my listening and analyzing mode, Isabel continues the work. "I guess the only thing worse than the fact that I'm unconsciously trying to manipulate you into reassuring me is what happens when you refuse," Isabel rejoins. "I'm just beginning to see how furious and disappointed I feel when I don't get what I want and need from you and from other people around me. I suppose my tears before and my saying I was a pessimist were as much out of anger as from sadness, a way of putting more pressure on you to say what I want you to say."

"And what would that be?"

"I'd want you to tell me I'm beautiful inside and out. But if you did, part of me would think I'd fooled you, that you don't really know me at all, because you'd be missing the angry manipulative side of me entirely. When you frustrate me like that it highlights just how big that angry and manipulative side really is. When you wouldn't say what I wanted you to say, I had a thought that shows just how mean I can really be." Isabel pauses, swallows hard, and looks embarrassed, anxious. "I thought that your hair could certainly use some of that conditioner that I was looking for in the dream. It's looking kind of dull and frizzy." Isabel looks teary again. "So here I am trying to get you to tell me how good I am, what a nice person I am, and when you don't, I immediately start criticizing your hair, putting you down, proving in the process that I am in fact a terrible person after all."

Depending as an adult on the kindness of strangers (or even friends) to help us regulate our emotions and sense of self is doomed to fail for myriad reasons. First and foremost, others are ultimately beyond our control. So much of the time it simply doesn't work to depend on others to modulate our moods and our views of our self, because they fail or refuse to give us what we need. As this detailed dissection of my interaction with Isabel shows, when we fail in our efforts to elicit what we need from others, we are often left feeling frustrated and angry as well as having irritated the person we were trying to get a particular response from. Our interaction often hits a wall of mutual anger and comes to a dead stop.

Even when we do get what we need from them after all, the effects are temporary. Mood regulation is a moment-to-moment proposition. Aligning people in the world around us is like aligning the planets as they orbit the sun, a futile prospect to begin with. But even if we achieved it after lots of work, the alignment would only last a second before they slipped on by in their own orbits, eluding us once again. Furthermore, even when we elicit the response we need, our own inner emotional process tends to erode the ill-gotten goods. That compliment that we fished for is less fulfilling than we expect, in part because we fished for it, diminishing its value. Furthermore, because we realize at some level that how we feel inside is within the control of others, we tend to feel like biting the hand that feeds us, and this sense of angry ingratitude contributes to our pervasive sense of ourselves as bad. We're left feeling that we're not only manipulative and controlling but also ungrateful. Furthermore, we're aware that this is a part of ourselves that we don't want others to see. But hiding our inner badness then sets up a situation where others don't truly know us, and this means that even their unsolicited positive responses to us are suspect. We tend to feel like fakes or frauds—if only they knew who we really were, they'd feel as negatively about us as we do. This inner sense of being fraudulent in turn exacts a toll on our mood, since there is always the possibility that others will find out what we're really like inside. If that happened, on the one hand we'd be known, but on the other we'd be hated. The inner sense that to really know us is to hate us is the definition of low self-esteem.

It's easy to see how the world quickly becomes a dog-eat-dog place to Isabel, how her moods and her view of self and other contribute to her pessimistic outlook. When her attempt to modulate her mood and sense of self by eliciting the desired response from me doesn't work, the situation is even worse. Isabel becomes angry, frustrated, and attacking toward me for not giving her what she wants, and then imagines that I, in turn, will attack her. Her inner sense that she deserves an attack or a rejection from others is reflected in her view of the world—and people— around her, and how she experiences the world outside begins to mirror her inner sense of despair and dysregulation.

In the process of trying to control me, Isabel has indeed gotten me to be more controlling of her, more insistent about my own perspective, and more vocal in interpreting both what she is doing and why than I would usually be. It is only after her session ends that I come to realize that she has indeed made me feel like retaliating against her in response to her comment about my hair even though I have resisted doing so. As she leaves my office, I smooth my own unruly hair self-consciously while admiring her smooth, shiny locks. I feel unsettled, restless, disgruntled. It's a far different emotional state than the one I was in before Isabel walked into the room today. I let my mind wander to see what inner pictures of mine are connected to this feeling state. I picture the beautiful girl in the Breck commercial tossing her long, straight, blond hair to and fro. I recall how disappointing it was as a teenager to realize that I would never have hair like that. I feel a twinge of envy as I picture Isabel in the part. Her hair is definitely nicer than mine. She wins. I feel envious. For a moment I imagine getting back at her, cutting all her hair off the way I cut the hair on my sister's Barbie doll when I was seven. It started with me acting good and helpful. "Oh, just let me give your doll's hair a trim." A little bit like my good and helpful but overly active and insistent remarks to Isabel today. But then Barbie's hair is never quite even, and in an attempt to even it out I make it shorter and shorter. I can still picture the look on my sister's face when I returned her bald Barbie. So much for the hostility behind the helpfulness. And I may feel similarly toward Isabel as well, helpful on the surface and annoyed underneath, my annoyance a natural and common response to some faint inner awareness of being psychologically manipulated and controlled by her. As I arrive at a better understanding of the meaning of my fleeting fantasy about cropping Barbie's blond locks, I feel my sense of annoyance and being disgruntled start to fade as I begin to understand what I am feeling and why, placing my reaction in its appropriate inter-personal context. But suppose I hadn't been inter-ested in or able to makes these connections, to hold back on acting on my feelings until I understood them. Isn't it likely that I would subtly attack Isabel instead, as many people seem to, in the process prob-ably proving to her that her pessimistic view of her-self, others, and the world was actually warranted? It's easy to see how her attempts to control others back-fire and contribute to the very sense of dysregulation that they are designed to fix.

These kinds of subtle interpersonal maneuvers and the feelings that they generate happen all the time, hidden transactions between people, which op-erate just out of awareness. Because I believe Isabel is acting in response to an internalized relationship model that she doesn't yet understand, I believe that she is not yet cognizant of either her attempts to con-trol me or how those attempts unfold. Thus, in say-ing she is trying to elicit a given reaction from me, I do not mean to imply that she is being purposefully or consciously manipulative, only that she is caught in the sway of a particular way of relating to others that she has learned, a way that depends on control-ling them in order to produce within herself the positive feelings and self-concept that she cannot generate on her own. And the only thing that's different about what happens between me and Isabel and what happens with people all the time as we move about in the world is that Isabel and I are trying to understand the hidden transactions between us that shape our moment-to-moment feelings, our views of ourselves and our perspectives on other people. The difference is not in the interaction itself but in the analysis of it.

Perhaps as I've talked in the last three chapters about cortico-limbic loops and their childhood development as well as the problems that early life experiences can leave us with in later life, you've been feeling increasingly pessimistic. After all, if optimism in later life depends on brain circuitry that evolves in the first several years, what can be done if it develops incorrectly? If your first three years didn't go so well, what now? You might be tempted to blame Mom or to throw up your hands in despair. But to do so would amount to the very "victim" mentality that leads us to surrender not only responsibility for ourselves but also our capacity to take charge of the situation. And if there is one take-home lesson about optimism that you've derived thus far, I hope it's that to foster an optimistic stance, we must find ways to maximize our sense of control over ourselves and the world around us. In the next chapter we'll look at what you can do to change how you feel and how you see yourself, how you can gain real control over your own inner states of mind. Even if you're feeling half empty like Isabel right now, with effort you can become a self in full.

Chapter Seven

STRATEGIES FOR SEEING THE GLASS HALF FULL

IF EARLY LIFE interactions with others have left you feeling half empty, with less than optimal cortico-limbic circuitry for optimism, what can you do about it now? How can an adult whose perspective is more pessimistic than they would like change, become a full self? In this chapter, I'll explore how Eeyore can change his gray and pessimistic mood, becoming more like his vibrant and bouncy friend Tigger instead. The answers are based in part on my own clinical research findings and also stem from an in-depth understanding of how our cortico-limbic loops operate and what we can do to make them work more effectively in our favor.

Our cortico-limbic loops operate to help us regulate our own states of mind, but they can be easily overridden by disorders such as depression, manic depression, panic attacks, and other anxiety disorders. When these disorders are present, our attempts to make our cortico-limbic loops function more effectively to modulate our inner states may be futile, like trying to keep control of a surf board amid a typhoon. When caught in the grip of more serious forms of mood dysregulation, often the most prudent course of action—and the one most likely to promote a more optimistic perspective—is to take a medication designed to place the nature and intensity of our emotional responses back in the right range.

If we're struggling with real chronic depression, medications such as the new classes of ssri antidepressants can shift the nature and intensity of our emotions back into the right range. With a hoist in the right direction, we can then hope to take back the reins for ourselves.

My own research at Columbia, a long-term study of patients in psychotherapy and psychoanalysis who were and were not on medication, indicates that there are a significant number of people with definitive mood and anxiety disorders who do not choose the benefit of antidepressant or anti-anxiety drugs but for whom medication is clinically indicated. Contrary to the quick-fix view many people have of cosmetic pharmacology, my colleagues and I found that it was the use of the drugs themselves that correlated with a willingness to stick it out in talk therapy.

Patients who chose not to take drugs though they had substantial, demonstrable depression and anxiety (measured on specific psychiatric scales) seemed unable or unwilling to tolerate the painful process that intensive talk therapy can often become. These were the patients who quit. Furthermore, during the time that those patients who needed but weren't on medication suffered bouts of depression, they were less psychologically minded (and thus presumably less capable of working well in therapy which depends on the capacity to see the psychological motives behind behaviors). When depressed or anxious these patients also tended to see events around them as beyond their control and themselves as less likely to have an impact on things (not the appropriate state for trying to get them to affect changes by understanding their own contribution to their problems). Indeed, when their depressive or anxiety symptoms remitted, they were more likely to feel that they had an impact on what happened to them, less at the mercy of the world, as well as becoming more psychologically minded.[1]

The impact of medication for mood disorders is also clear in looking at the reactions of rats who experienced early life separations. When placed in an environment in which their choices were to cower behind a bunker or search among wood chips in an open area of their cages for Cocoa Crispies (which are apparently like ambrosia to rats), rats who had a history of early life separations cowered. When placed on the antidepressant Paxil, they searched for Cocoa Crispies with the best of them. Taken off Paxil, they returned to cowering. For many people (and rats as well), if you want to get the Cocoa Crispies life has to offer, medication can help.

These findings about the importance of mood disorders are not surprising once we consider that given a contest between the control that the cortex attempts to exert over the limbic system in modulating our moods and a limbic system in disarray amidst a significant depressive or anxiety disorder, the limbic system disarray will overwhelm the cortical controls every time. Even though we consider the cortex king, the fact is that lower brain areas are far older in evolutionary terms, and often a disturbance at a lower level cannot be rectified at a higher level. Although we tend to think of the cortex as more advanced, if the so-called more primitive areas of the brain responsible for breathing stop functioning, there is nothing the cortex can do about it. The lower limbic system has direct inputs to the brain stem nuclei that regulate norepinephrine, serotonin, and dopamine, and if it malfunctions, there is similarly likely to be little we can do about it by using our cortex alone.

But for every person who is positively affected by medication for mood and anxiety symptoms, there is another who is disappointed to find that medication does not solve their problems completely. While medication can be essential in putting our mood or anxiety levels back in the right ballpark, after that it's up to us to hone the skills we need to effectively modulate our emotions within their normal bounds, and medication cannot generally accomplish this task for us. Even when we are not depressed or anxious in a pathological way, there are moment-to-moment fluxes in our moods based in part on the representations of self and other active at the time. We all need to know how to handle such feelings as sadness, anxiety, shame, and elation. The more we understand what types of inner representations and outer situations trigger these emotions, the more we'll know how these moods affect our sense of self and our view of the world around us, and the better positioned we'll be to buffer their effects.

Another important route in increasing optimism is to learn tactics that will make our current cortico-limbic loops, existing as they do right now, work more effectively. In thinking about what types of maneuvers are likely to be useful, it may help to go back to the anatomy of the limbic system itself, with the amygdala sandwiched like a sentinel between the constantly chattering cortex that sits above it, and the continual influx of sensory information bubbling up to it from the world around us and our own bodies. The cortical pathway suggests that we can change how we feel by changing what we think, while the stream of incoming sensory information suggests that by bathing ourselves in various soothing sensations we might pacify the limbic system.

The notion that we can change *what* we feel by changing *how* we think has a long and distinguished history that dates back to Aristotle. He said that we experience events as good or bad according to our evaluations of them. In other words, the cortex would serve as the grand master, the judge that would determine how the lowly limbic system should make us feel about the world around us. Shakespeare echoed this understanding when he wrote in *Hamlet* that "there is nothing either good or bad but thinking makes it so." Similarly, in *The Passions of the Soul*, Descartes argues that emotions arise in the thinking aspect of ourselves and can be controlled by our thoughts. Freud spoke of the rider atop the horse, controlling his direction, where the rider was the ego (the seat of logic and realism), while the horse was the id (the seat of unbridled aggressive and sexual drives) that the rider struggled to hold in check.[2] In fact, there is much from psychological research to demonstrate that, indeed, thinking does make it so. But exactly how should we think to achieve optimism?

It turns out that there are specific ways of thinking about events that tend to either maximize our sense of luck and power or to rip the reins of control right out of our hands.[3] Let's say that you just cannot seem to make a computer program work, no matter what you do. Like an unsolvable anagram, an uncontrollable shock, or an insidious noise that we cannot eliminate, even this kind of simple, everyday problem can lead to a sense of frustrated helplessness, personal incompetence, and loss of control. But whether or not we will have this reaction depends primarily on how we explain the failure to ourselves and, perhaps more importantly, what we think that failure says about who we really are. People who tend toward pessimism cannot sustain a positive inner state and the illusion of control over the world. Thus, when a computer program fails to work, they tend to tell themselves that "Computer programs *never* work for me" and that "I'm having trouble with this program because *all* computer programs are too difficult." And worst of all, pessimists tend to believe that they are to blame for the problem, that the failure is all their fault. So they might think, "I couldn't make the program work because I'm dumb." But you'd expect this way of looking at the world, looking at things in global and pervasive terms and relating everything to the self, to stand the pessimist in good stead when good things happen. You'd expect them to think that if the computer program *did* work, it would mean that they were computer savvy in a universal and en- during way and that they and they alone were re- sponsible for their success. But with pessimists the bad news just keeps getting worse. When success strikes, they actually switch their pattern of thinking around, seeing good events as the result of temporary, nonenduring flukes and explaining successes in ways that lessen their impact. Thus, they explain that "The computer worked today because I was lucky" or "I'm just good with this one program," limiting the duration and scope of their ability to exert control and, in the process, limiting the mood lift that should accompany their success. In addition, such people are likely to explain good outcomes as the result of external factors: "I could run the program because it was so user-friendly." But because people with mood regulatory problems often feel half empty, with a negative view of themselves predominating, then the way they are looking at defeats and successes actually makes logical sense. Their bad self can predictably produce negative results, whereas good outcomes from a bad self would seem aberrant and fluky, beyond their control, because how could a bad self produce positive results anyway?

The same is true of the thought patterns of people whose mood-modulatory abilities make them more optimistic. Based on their predominantly positive view of themselves, they tend to see setbacks and bad events as related to temporary conditions and specific problems. In response to a failure on the computer, they're more likely to say "*Today* was a bad day for me with the computer" or "I can't do it because *this* computer program is too difficult." In essence, they are limiting the domain of their failure to something temporary and specific, a problem today with this particular program. When they fail, these folks also tend to believe that the failure is not their fault. Instead, they think that "The program didn't work because *it's* dumb" or "Its instructions were lacking." When good events happen, they tend to see the good events that befall them as the result of positive, permanent, and enduring aspects of themselves. So when success strikes, you'll find them thinking "I'm usually talented with computers" or noting to themselves that "I can make lots of different programs work." And, of course, they're apt to take credit for the success, believing that "I got the program to work quickly because I'm smart." In other words, because they see themselves as predominantly good, they see good outcomes as the result of the impact of the good and successful self, and bad events as the fluke.

Not surprisingly, research has also shown that those with what Martin Seligman and colleagues have dubbed an optimistic explanatory style tend to see positive attributes as more characteristic of themselves than negative ones. They show poorer recall for episodes in which they failed than for those in which they succeeded, remembering their performances on various tasks to be more positive and successful than they actually were. In addition, they tend to view their lesser capabilities as common and less valuable than those areas in which they excel, which they tend to view as rare, distinctive, and especially valuable attributes. In other words, what they are proficient at is perceived by them as more important than what they are not proficient at. When informed that an ability is valued by others, they tend to perceive that they already possess or have improved their skills in that area through practice, even when outside raters believe that their skills remain unchanged, unimproved. Finally, they give others less credit for their successes yet more blame for their failures than people who are less effective mood modulators, seeing themselves as both better than average and as better than others see them. In contrast, people who have a more pessimistic explanatory style recall their own positive and negative attributes with an equal valence, showing an evenhandedness in attributing their shortcomings to themselves versus other people and demonstrating greater congruence between how they rate themselves on various attributes and how those around them rate them. What all this evenhandedness ultimately gets them is a view of the self that reflects their inner sense of badness as well as the preponderance of negative emotions and the sense of lack of self-control that accompanies it. Although those with a so-called optimistic style are clearly distorting reality (or at least others' perspectives on them), they are ultimately distorting reality in the service of maximizing their sense of well-being, bolstering their self-esteem, and enhancing their illusions of control.[4]

Looking at the different thought patterns of people who sustain an optimistic perspective and those who do not suggests that perhaps shifting your thought patterns could also shift how you feel, including how you feel about yourself. In other words, if you find yourself explaining a success in specific, temporary, and external terms, repeatedly dissecting and rationally challenging the thought and recasting it in the terms in which an optimist would naturally see a success—as global, permanent, and the result of personal talent—this can gradually chip away at long-ingrained cortical patterns and gradually replace pessimism with optimism. The premise is simple but profound; train yourself to think like an optimist and you will gradually become one, with a resultant improvement in your moods and your view of yourself and others. When you try to begin thinking about good events like an optimist—seeing them as the result of positive global persistent attributes of your self over which you exert control—you are ultimately trying to alter your sense of self in relation to other people. Rather than thinking that you are less talented or accomplished or can never do anything right—perspectives that belittling, shaming, or derogatory caretakers might foster in early life (perhaps to bolster their *own* flagging sense of self), you are gradually learning to see yourself differently as well as to regulate your mood more effectively in a manner that permits optimism.

A second way of altering our thinking that has been shown to promote an upbeat mood, and the optimistic perspective that accompanies it, is known as downward comparison. Consider the following simple but elegant study. A group of subjects were randomly divided into two subgroups. One group of subjects was asked to complete the sentence "I'm glad I'm not a…" five times. The other group was asked to complete the sentence "I wish I were a…" five times. Each group rated how satisfied they felt with their lives before the sentence-completion task and again later, after they had finished the task. The group of subjects who completed the "I'm glad I'm not a…" sentence were markedly more satisfied with their lives afterwards, whereas those who completed the "I wish I were a…" sentence rated themselves as significantly more dissatisfied than they had been merely minutes earlier.[5] Because our emotions occur in the context of relationships between ourselves and others, comparing ourselves with those who are less well off helps us to create and sustain the illusion that we are fortunate. This sense that we stack up favorably in turn buoys our mood in a more positive direction. In contrast, comparing ourselves with others who are better off and have things that we desire tends to make us feel envious and to create feelings of angry deprivation and frustration, ultimately displacing us from a position of emotional equilibrium and making us less satisfied with our plight.

Once again the ability or inability to generate this kind of thinking on our own depends upon our view of our self and our current state of emotional regulation or dysregulation. Nondepressed cancer patients were observed to generate positive feelings by reasoning that their illness could have been worse or comparing themselves to someone whose illness was actually worse. But under the weight of depression and anxiety, the ability to sustain this illusion of being relatively fortunate compared to other cancer patients quickly collapsed.[6] In fact, people with mild chronic depression typically fail to exhibit self-protective social comparisons with others, but when researchers were able to enhance such self-protective comparisons, the subjects' moods improved.[7]

As useful as these two methods of adjusting our

thinking—adopting a more positive attributional style and making downward comparisons—may be in helping us more effectively regulate our mood, you may find them distasteful. After all, if I flunk a math test, then claim—in keeping with an external explanation for my failure—that the professor's exam was unfair, where's my sense of personal responsibility for the fact that I simply didn't study? Interestingly, while this post hoc explanation for why I failed may sound obnoxiously abdicating of all responsibility, people who adopt this attributional style actually study harder for the next test. Of course, this makes sense because they see good outcomes as generally within their ability to control and expect their studying to pay off in a good grade. Thus, their explanation of the failed exam is unlikely to degenerate into the abdication of all responsibility. Rather, their explanation protects them from feelings of failure, and that protection in turn permits them to study harder the next time around.

In terms of downward comparison, if I constantly look for others who are worse off and use their misery to bolster my sense of self, how do I keep from feeling guilty? Interestingly, those who sustain the illusion of being relatively fortunate in some ways by capitalizing on the misfortune of others are also more likely than those who do not make such comparisons to volunteer or engage in altruistic activities.[8] In other words, they are likely to try to change the plight of those less fortunate, in the process obviating any feelings of guilt they might have for the kinds of comparisons they make. People who volunteer their time and energy to causes they consider worthwhile are often happier and more optimistic with an improved sense of self-esteem in response to their volunteerism. In a sense, they may be modeling the benevolent caretaker who assisted them in early life when they were unable to help themselves and generating part of the sense of happiness surrounding that caretaking relationship. Even the Dalai Lama admits to using downward comparison—accompanied by the appropriate amount of altruistic assistance of others, of course—to bolster his feelings of happiness and contentedness with his own situation.[9]

Changing attributional style and making downward comparisons are ways of modulating the limbic system via the cortex. There are also equally valid ways of having the desired impact on our moods by altering the nature of the incoming stream of sensory input from our bodies and the world around us, which constantly bathes the amygdala. Perhaps the most striking optimism-inducing research is that which provides a sure shortcut: If you don't feel it, fake it. Consider the surprising results of the following studies. Native German speakers were asked to read four two-hundred-word stories, two of which had a high frequency of the vowel *u* (like the English "oo"). In order to pronounce this vowel, the readers lips must protrude, the exact opposite facial expression of smiling. The subjects who read the two stories with the high frequency of the vowel *u* registered a dislike of the stories even though they were similar in content to the non-*u* stories. Their attitude toward the stories was apparently altered by the facial expression involved in the reading itself because the repeated frowning the *u* sound produced sent a particular kind of bodily input to their limbic systems, which in turn altered their moods. By making scowling faces, they developed scowling attitudes.[10]

Similarly, when subjects were asked to hold a pen in their mouths in another study, causing them to inadvertently make the facial muscle movements more characteristic of a smile, they rated cartoons as more funny than did subjects not contracting these muscles. When subjects were induced to mimic a sad face by drawing their eyebrows together, they then judged pictures to be more sad than subjects who did not mimic such a face, even though they were unaware that it was the facial expression itself that was producing the emotional reaction.[11] These studies suggest that your mother was right when she advised you to put on a happy face. (Of course, perhaps they also suggest that you shouldn't listen to her when she tells you not to chew on that smile-inducing pencil.) But the bottom line is that by acting happier, even if it initially feels fake, you can gradually begin to feel happier as well. Sit up straight and you will likely feel less tired. Relax your muscles (and the inputs they send your limbic system) and you will feel less anxious. And the reverse can also be true: inhibiting facial displays of negative emotions can actually help reduce the intensity of the emotion we experience. So acting stoic in the face of a painful medical procedure can actually make the feelings of fear and pain less powerful.[12]

While there is a powerful link between facial expression and emotion, other kinds of external stimulation, such as having our skin touched and stroked through massage or cuddling, looking at tranquil scenes, smelling pleasant smells, or listening to various kinds of mood-affecting music, are other useful ways of altering the limbic system's state from below. Because of their ability to evoke emotions (perhaps conjuring up the vitality affects that Stern suggests are so important in early communication between people) arts like music and dance may be uniquely suited to alter the limbic tone from below.

But be forewarned that you can defeat this kind of modulation of the amygdala by having a cortex that continues to spin dark scenarios or to ruminate instead of relaxing. If you get a massage while mulling over the reasons for your poor work review, chances are that you will override any positive limbic effects of the massage with the mulling, leaving your limbic system stewing rather than subdued.

You should also be aware that, not surprisingly, the effect of external stimuli on the limbic system can also work for the worse. For instance, in one study of the effects of different types of music, 144 subjects completed a psychological profile before and after listening for fifteen minutes to four types of music. Those who were forced to listen to grunge rock showed significant increases in hostility, sadness, tension, and fatigue, and significant reductions were observed in caring, relaxation, mental clarity, and vigor. So it pays to pay attention to what's happening in the world around you and, to the extent possible, to modify it so that it has the desired impact on your mood.[13]

One special subset of stimuli in the world around

us that can definitely have an impact on the state of our limbic systems is other people. One of the primary reasons that we have emotions in the first place is that they send signals to others, serving as a means of communication as well as a way of facilitating social bonds. Our facility at reading and responding to the emotions of those around us also makes us especially susceptible to picking up on and being influenced by the moods of those around us. In short, emotions are contagious, as every psychiatrist knows when they try to schedule a manic rather than a depressed patient for the end of their day so that they leave the office singing show tunes rather than dirges. If you've ever seen a nursery of babies, you know that when one cries, they all cry. Understanding the strength of this person-to-person effect allows us to harness other people's emotional reactions in a manner that positively affects our moods, as when we bounce a smile or a friendly attitude to them and, most often, they return it, sometimes magnified, to us. It's a kind of person-to-person mood Ping-Pong and, like other external stimuli, it works in both directions. That means you may want to think twice before cursing at that cab driver and unleashing his stream of abusive and angry comments, with its ability to adversely affect your mood.

While these cortical and sensory tactics may help the cortico-limbic loops we have in place right now to function optimally, for some people these tricks of the trade are simply not enough to make a long-standing difference in how they feel or to give them a firm sense of controlling their own emotional states. In such cases, the solution that most promotes optimism may be intensive psychotherapy or psychoanalysis. Just as experience in early life shapes the way that neurons in the limbic areas and cortex are interconnected, later life exploration of the relationship patterns we have internalized, as well as their emotional consequences, can result in changes in the ways in which neurons are interconnected. This rewiring leads in turn to changes in how relationships and the emotions attached to them are experienced and integrated, to a reworking of our view of ourselves and others and the emotional ties that connect us. By physically changing the circuitry of the cortico-limbic loops themselves as well as understanding what about their prior organization was problematic, we can literally change our minds and moods.

Decades before we arrived at our understanding of cortico-limbic circuitry, Freud suggested the idea of stereotype plates, patterns based on our early experiences that are indelibly etched upon our brains and repeatedly invoked as models when we interact with others. As I explained in chapter 4, the stories we tell about interactions between ourselves and others are remarkably parallel regardless of whether they are made up or real, from the past or present, from dreams or waking life, stories about a therapist, or stories about others. So if stories from childhood revolve around themes of victimization and being belittled and humiliated, stories about current relationships tend to have this same theme, too. There is also evidence that over time in psychotherapy, the relationship patterns and expectations driving each individual's unique story line can be changed, with a resultant positive shift in a patient's view of himself in relation to others as well as an improved ability to understand and modulate his own emotional states. Indeed, psychotherapy researchers have found that the stories people tell later on in psychotherapy are less stereotyped and less rigidly adherent to the same core patterns and that these shifts in the story patterns are actually correlated with a reduction in depressive and anxiety symptoms as well.[15] The exploration of these patterns in psychotherapy, including in the ever unfolding relationship with the therapist, gradually gives rise to actual shifts in the way the neurons that form the cortico-limbic loops are interconnected, with a resultant change in the way that those circuits process information. We gradually alter our view of ourselves and others and the emotional tones that characterize our connections. But what happens in psychotherapy that allows us to improve our capacity for mood modulation and thereby increase our self-esteem? First, in psychotherapy people attend—sometimes for the first time ever—to what their emotional states actually are. One result of all this monitoring of one's own inner states is that emotional states often become increasingly differentiated through the process of therapy. As in a music education class where what was once just a quartet suddenly seems recognizable as a violin and flute and two cellos, people who once described feeling diffusely "upset" slowly become able to identify the blend of anger and anxiety that they are actually feeling. A second effect of psychotherapy is to give us an improved understanding of what makes our inner states shift from moment to moment. Because we observe the flow of thoughts and fantasies and sensations that accompany shifts in our emotional states, we begin to understand what contributes to shifting them in a given direction. This careful attention to the unfolding of our inner process can lead us ultimately to understand our relationship patterns and expectations. For Isabel in the last chapter, her covert criticism of my hair in response to my failure to reassure her, triggered feelings of guilt and personal badness. This type of pattern is repeated again and again in her relationships; the only difference is that when it happens with me, she has an opportunity to explore and understand it. So just as we might begin to understand a chord progression in a piece of music, in psychotherapy we gradually become able to dissect and deconstruct the flow of our inner states of mind in a manner that allows us to understand our moods. This insight ultimately gives us more capacity to control our emotions as we grow better at understanding their sources and origins. Although knowing what we feel and why are crucially important steps in bettering our ability to modulate our emotions, psychotherapy actually provides an opportunity for something even more crucial. Because the exploration of our inner states occurs in the context of the relationship with our therapist, psychotherapy actually gives us the chance for a new affective apprenticeship.[16]

Just as our caretakers served as the external regulators of our inner states in childhood, the relationship with a therapist who is equally attentive to all of our feelings, good and bad, can give us another opportunity to develop a more positive and autonomous view of our self that comes from internalizing this new experience of a relationship. We learned that secure attachments evolve when parents attend to and tolerate all of a child's feelings without privileging certain emotions or asking the child to suppress how he feels. If the affective apprenticeship of early life went awry, psychotherapy offers a second chance to develop a broader affective range as well as an improved capacity to regulate the intensity and nature of our emotional experiences for ourselves. There is interesting evidence that this is indeed how people use the relationship with the therapist. For instance, one study showed that 90% of patients engaged in weekly outpatient psychotherapy thought about their therapist between sessions. Interestingly, when researchers asked in detail when the representation of the therapist was evoked, patients reported that they pictured and thought about their therapist most vividly when they were attempting to mitigate painful feelings like sadness, anxiety, depression, and guilt. Patients said that they evoked the image of the therapist most at those particular moments to help themselves feel less alone, less anxious or depressed, less overwhelmed, and more connected.[17] As with young children who sing songs they usually sing with mother to lessen the impact of a separation and the painful feelings it invokes, by conjuring the connection with the therapist in his absence, patients seem to use what they have internalized about the relationship to mitigate painful states of mind more effectively for themselves. Therapists help patients stretch their capacity for elation and joy as well as showing them that they—and their relationship to the therapist—do not die or disintegrate when they experience intense anger, anxiety, sadness, shame, or excitement. They help the patient to repair rifts in the relationship—and in his own self-esteem—when it is ruptured, in the process making the patient's view of himself more resilient. This process of emotional conditioning in therapy gradually reshapes the early life lessons that the cortico-limbic loops have reified in their circuitry.

In the end, as Isabel's dream in the last chapter suggested, the true goal of therapy is to make us more autonomous, more able to count on our own inner island. We don't want to have to depend on others to provide us with the conditioners we need to unsnarl our inner states; we want to make them for ourselves. It is only when we have this autonomous ability that our preponderance of negative feelings, our sense of being unable to control them and the harsh and self-critical view of the self that so naturally follows can be transformed, allowing us to become a self in full.

Chapter Eight

A MASTER
ILLUSIONIST
IN ACTION

ONCE WE HAVE ACHIEVED THE AUTONOMY that accompanies becoming a self in full, we can count on ourselves to sustain optimism even when our illusion of having mastered the world that whirls around us is shattered by events beyond our control. Still, to Jean-Dominique Bauby, having a stroke must have felt like hitting a brick wall doing sixty.[1] He writes:

> I am functioning in slow motion, and in the beam of the headlights I barely recognize turns I have negotiated several thousand times. I feel sweat beading my forehead, and when I overtake a car I see it double. At the first intersection, I pull over. I stagger from the BMW, almost unable to stand

upright, and collapse on the rear seat....And then I sink into a coma.

The editor-in-chief of French *Elle,* Bauby was a successful man in his early forties and the father of two young children. He was well regarded by colleagues and friends, who valued his wit, style, and impassioned approach to life. Bauby was literally behind the wheel one day, speeding to pick up his son for the weekend, when he began to feel woozy, dizzy, not himself. The next thing he knew, it was twenty days later and he awoke to find he was the victim of "locked-in" syndrome following a massive stroke. He was paralyzed from head to toe, unable to move except for blinking his left eye. But he had normal bodily sensation and his mind was left entirely intact, able to take in the whole situation. Undoubtedly, he had lots to say about his plight, but his means of communication were severely limited because of his paralysis. "In one flash I saw the frightening truth," he was to write later about the moment when the extent of his injuries actually sunk in. "It was as blinding as an atomic explosion and keener than a guillotine blade." He could not speak or sign or even shake his head yes or no.

Luckily for Bauby, that blinding, sharp-edged

flash of insight about his state was quickly replaced by a determination to make himself heard nonetheless. Like the breast cancer patients who shifted their thinking about what they were in control of when their cancer recurred, Bauby looked for and found the one window through which to influence the world around him that wasn't closed by his brain injury. He learned that when his visitors said the alphabet slowly, letter by letter, he could blink his left eye as they passed the letter he wanted and thereby painstakingly spell out words and sentences to make himself understood. Even when a catastrophic stroke shattered his illusion of being at the wheel, literally taking away virtually all control over his own body, he found the one lifeline to the world outside that still existed and took charge of using it for all it was worth. In fact, he later used the eye-blink technique to write a book, *The Diving-Bell and the Butterfly*. If you can imagine doing the same in his position, congratulations. Your cortico-limbic loops must be as finely sculpted as Atlas's washboard abs.

Bauby's desire to continue to have an impact on the world around him is impressive. But his book's title hints that the type of control most important to him was mastery of his emotions. Even when his whole body was weighed down, held prisoner by what he called a giant diving bell, Bauby could let his mind take flight

> like a butterfly. There is so much to do. You can wander off in space or in time, set out for the Tierra del Fuego or for King Midas's court. You can visit the woman you love, slide down beside her, and stroke her still-sleeping face. You can build castles in Spain, steal the Golden Fleece, discover Atlantis, realize your childhood dreams and adult ambitions.

Bauby quickly came to realize the importance of what I have argued in this book—that the one thing we can all potentially have control over in times of duress is the content and the climate of our own inner world. And he began to see that it was this sense of being at the helm of his own inner world that helped the world around him seem welcoming as well, despite his massive injuries.

In the last chapter, I argued that taking charge of our inner world requires an understanding of what we are feeling and why, and then using all the means at our disposal to move our state of mind in the desired direction. Rather than letting our limbic system control us, we have to learn to exercise maximal control over it. It is this process of taking charge of our inner state that permits us to be master illusionists when it comes to shaping our perception of the world around us as well. Too often those who surrender self-control and adopt the pessimistic stance that comes with such an abdication have decided—consciously or unconsciously—to treat life as a documentary in which they are buffeted about by external forces and are merely observing rather than directing and determining their perspective on themselves and the world around them. After all, even documentaries are not pure reality, they have a perspective, a take on the tale being told. The camera is being pointed at something while avoiding looking directly at something else. There is editing, with its inherent choices about what to focus on. I am suggesting that optimists instead treat life as a story they direct, whose focus they determine, more like a fictive feature film than a documentary. When it comes to directing one's life story, Bauby is a master illusionist, able to rewrite the script of his newly constrained existence. Through some crucial directorial decisions, Bauby enables himself to focus much more on the butterflies of his existence than its diving bells, making his life more satisfying and in the process exerting more real impact on the people around him.

We saw in the last chapter that shifting the focus of our thinking can help us as we struggle to master our moods. Bauby is a master director of his own mind, determining where he focuses his attention, just as a filmmaker determines where to point the camera. Look how well this technique works in an essay from Bauby's book, entitled "My Lucky Day":

> This morning, with first light barely bathing Room 119, evil spirits descended on my world. For half an hour, the alarm on the machine that regulates my feeding tube has been beeping out into the void. I cannot imagine anything so inane or nerve-racking as this piercing beep beep beep pecking away at my brain. As a bonus, my sweat has unglued the tape that keeps my right eyelid closed and the stuck-together lashes are tickling my pupil unbearably. And to crown it all, the end of my urinary catheter has become detached and I am drenched. Awaiting rescue, I hum an old song by Henri Salvador: "Don't you fret, baby, it'll be all right." And here comes the nurse. Automatically she turns on the TV. A commercial, with a personal computer spelling out the question: "Were you born lucky?"

You'd think that if anyone might lie there and whimper like a helpless hound, it'd be Bauby. After all, even the uncontrollable noise of his beeping feeding tube sounds like just the kind of torture researchers might dream up to create learned helplessness. Bauby finds himself in a position that would make most of us depressed, angry, anxious, despondent, even suicidal. What happens to people in situations where their helplessness seems to be inescapable? The strategies Bauby uses to avoid feelings of helplessness can be usefully employed by everyone as they grapple with intense emotions.[2] Bauby refocuses his mind on a comforting song designed to nudge his thinking away from the real-life physical sensations he is actually having. By venturing inward in search of something soothing, he finds the message he most needs to hear at the moment: "Don't you fret, baby, it'll be all right." The music and its words soothe him, putting him in a calmer, maybe even contented mood while he awaits rescue. In effect, he is not merely lying there waiting for the aversive shock to end, he is ending it himself by putting its sensations aside. In the process, he manages to dispel the evil spirits that have descended upon his room—a metaphor, perhaps, for the shadows of frightened, frustrated, or angry moods that threaten his state of mind—by humming a familiar song. He creates the inner environment that he needs to be at home within himself in a difficult moment by using his thought processes to pull his mood back into a more comfortable place.

Clearly, turning his focus away from his physical misery is important. But what Bauby directs his mind *toward* is as important as what he shifts it away from. When he is not caught up in a flight of fancy, building castles in Spain or stealing the Golden Fleece, he is reaching into his memory for experiences from the past that are likely to bring him from an inner state of boredom or loneliness into one of engagement and excitement. Fantasy and memory— the imagined future and the remembered past—are prime tools we can use to transport ourselves into alternative states of mind, affecting an emotional getaway. For Bauby this allowed him to write a book of what he affectionately refers to as "bedridden travel notes," a phrase that stresses both the reality of his diving bell and the equally important existence of his mental journeys. He writes:

> Fortunately I have stored away enough pictures, smells, and sensations over the course of the years to enable me to leave [the hospital] far behind.... They are strange wanderings: The sour smell of a New York bar. The odor of poverty in a Rangoon market. Little bits of the world. The white icy

nights of Saint Petersburg or the unbelievably molten sun at Furnace Creek in the Nevada desert.

He even describes the process of using memory to alter his mood in terms of the movies:

> Suddenly in my own personal movie theater, the forgotten footage of a spring weekend began to unroll....

As most pessimists are well aware, simply shifting what we are thinking about does not necessarily change in a productive way how we feel. Memories can be painful as well as pleasurable, as Bauby acknowledges when he writes that his weekly bath creates

> nostalgia for the protracted immersions that were the joy of my previous life. Armed with a cup of tea or a Scotch, a good book or a pile of newspapers, I would soak for hours, maneuvering the taps with my toes. Rarely do I feel my condition so cruelly as when I am recalling such pleasures. Luckily I have no time for gloomy thoughts. Already they are wheeling me back, shivering, to my room.

Because feelings and thoughts are so interconnected, allowing ourselves to focus for too long on gloomy thoughts can only lead our feelings in the same direction, and self-pity is one of the emotional states likely to make us the unhappiest and least optimistic of all.

That's why Bauby seems to frequently engage in downward comparison, focusing his attention on those who are in a similar situation to his own or even less well off, comparing himself to Alexandre Dumas's Noirtier de Villefort in *The Count of Monte Cristo,* a living mummy three quarters of the way into the grave, who spends his life in a wheelchair, also communicating by blinking. (Villefort, like Bauby, apparently suffers from locked-in syndrome.) Surrounded by such company, Bauby can easily feel that others are equally unfortunate, even if his locked-in friend is purely fictional. And when he thinks of the "score of comatose patients, patients at death's door, plunged into endless night" who never leave their rooms at the hospital, he notes that they "weigh strangely on our collective awareness, almost like a guilty conscience." His guilt probably arises from comparing his favorable situation to those less fortunate and feeling some sense of relief that he is in fact lucky by comparison. But if Bauby chose instead to focus on the "tourists," as he calls those merely undergoing rehab at the hospital who are expected to recover completely, or if he continued to compare his present condition to himself prior to the accident, sipping Scotch as he soaked in the bath, he would likely feel angry and embittered, chasing his optimistic perspective away in the process. Bauby seems to inherently understand that downward comparison with those less fortunate is a trick that really works to make ourselves feel lucky, while upward comparison with those who have more than we do can easily stir difficult-to-manage feelings of anger, envy, and injustice that can make our moods black instead.

Another trick of thought that Bauby frequently utilizes is that of rewriting scenes in his mind to give them different endings. This technique serves him well as a method of repairing the damage done to his ego by unfortunate encounters and events. Consider Bauby's reaction to the eye surgeon who sews his right eye shut to prevent it from eroding Bauby's cornea without ever bothering to explain what he is doing and why:

> I have known gentler awakenings. When I came to that late-January morning, the hospital ophthalmologist was leaning over me and sewing my right eyelid shut with a needle as if he were darning a sock. Irrational terror swept over me. What if this man got carried away and sewed up my left eye as well, my only link to the outside world, the

184 Half Empty, Half Full

only window to my cell, the one tiny opening of my diving bell? In the tones of a prosecutor demanding a maximum sentence for a repeat offender, he barked out: "Six months!" I fired off a series of questioning signals with my working eye, but this man—who spent his days peering into people's pupils—was apparently unable to interpret a simple look.

So in order to fend off feelings of terror and help-lessness, Bauby simply gives the scene the ending that would restore himself to a more powerful position. When the ophthalmologist asks, "Do you see double?" Bauby takes pleasure in his imagined reply: "Yes, I see two assholes, not one." Of course, in the end, his retaliation is not merely imagined, recorded for posterity as it is in the pages of his book. Note that the power and control Bauby invests himself with in fantasy actually helps to heighten his illusion of control, his mastery over a difficult situation in the world around him, with an accompanying shift from negative to positive feelings.

In addition to focusing his thoughts in a manner that will positively influence how he feels, Bauby is also a master at adjusting the intensity of various sensory experiences as a second route to affecting the tone and climate of his inner world. Perhaps you recall how effective those luscious close-ups of straw-berries were in *Tess of the d'Urbervilles*. Or how much the sound of a heart pounding in the middle of a horror movie can boost your sense of trepidation. And whether the sensations are real and happening right now or merely reactivated as memories, Bauby is a master at capitalizing on their emotional impact and using it in the service of achieving the mood state he seeks. For instance, although Bauby is not al-lowed to eat because the muscles he needs to swallow are paralyzed, he reports that he has cultivated

the art of simmering memories....For pleasure, I have to turn to the vivid memory of tastes and smells, an inexhaustible reservoir of sensations. I treat myself to a dozen snails, a plate of Alsatian sausage with sauerkraut, a bottle of late-vintage golden Gewurtztraminer; or else I savor a simple soft-boiled egg with fingers of toast and lightly salted butter. What a banquet! The yolk flows warmly over my palate and down my throat. And indigestion is never a problem. Naturally I use the finest ingredients: the freshest vegetables, fish straight from the water, the most delicately marbled meat. Everything must be done right. Just to make sure, a friend sent me the recipe for authentic homemade sausage, andouillette de

Troyes, with three different kinds of meat braided in strips....Every slice melts a little on your tongue before you start chewing to extract all its flavor.

If your mouth is watering and your mood upbeat and expectant after these descriptions, you can see how focusing on intense sensory experiences is a means to induce the positive feelings that promote optimism. For Bauby such simmering memories surround him in a cloak of sensation that propels him away from the potential boredom and apathy of his tasteless real world.

In addition to intense moments in which our five senses are stimulated, movement and rhythm are external means to modulating our moods as well. While Bauby has lost the real-life ability to affect his physical reality, his ability to do it in fantasy remains vivid. He imagines himself "a Formula One driver... burning up the track...Stretched out on my bed—I mean, in my cockpit—I hurl myself into the corners, my head, weighed down by my helmet, wrenched painfully sideways by gravitational pull." By becoming a "Tour de France long shot on the verge of pulling off a record-setting victory" or "a phenomenal downhill skier" who can "still hear the roar of the crowd on the slope and the singing of the wind in my

ears," Bauby can escape into intense imagined or remembered experiences of movement and rhythm,
surrounding himself with the sensations that will sat-
isfy his need for excitement and adventure, boosting
his spirits accordingly.

Of course, physical sensations not only affect our
mood but activate specific thoughts, fantasies, and
memories as well. As Bauby puts it, "A domestic
event as commonplace as washing can trigger the
most varied emotions. One day, for example, I can
find it amusing in my forty-fifth year, to be cleaned
up and turned over, to have my bottom wiped and
swaddled like a newborn's. I even derive guilty pleasure from this total lapse into infancy. But the next
day, the same procedure seems to me unbearably sad,
and a tear rolls down through the lather a nurse's aide
spreads over my cheeks." So once again, it is the
choice to savor or avoid a sensation, according to its
effects on our inner state and capacity for optimism,
that must serve as the basis for our directorial decisions if the sensations we are engaged with are to
have the desired effect on our emotions.

Indeed, when Bauby realizes during his first trip
back to Paris after his stroke that he is made over-
whelmingly sad by his visit to the city he called
home, he actually "grays out" his sensory engagement

with its sights and sounds the next time he is there, distancing himself from the scenery and thus from the sad mood that he had experienced on his prior trip as well.

> What I saw through the ambulance window was just a movie background. Filmmakers call the process a "rear-screen projection," with the hero's car speeding along a road that unrolls behind him on a studio wall.…My own [second] crossing of Paris left me indifferent. Yet nothing was miss-ing—housewives in flowered dresses and youths on roller skates, revving buses, messengers cursing on their scooters. The Place de l'Opera, straight out of a Dufy canvas. The treetops foaming like surf against glass building fronts, wisps of cloud in the sky. Nothing was missing, except me. I was elsewhere.

Leaving the scene of intense sensation is a means of modulating the impact of the world around us on our inner state of being.

Not only can Bauby engage in soliloquies of thought and sensation to modulate his limbic system from above and below, but he also utilizes those around him. Bauby uses both the real people he in-teracts with and fantasies about others to create a sense of inner emotional comfort amid his ordeal.

For instance, Bauby's monthly letters about his progress to his friends often give him gratifying results. "Apart from an irrecoverable few who maintain a stubborn silence, everybody now understands that he can join me in my diving bell, even if sometimes the diving bell takes me into unexplored territory. I receive remarkable letters." Bauby is most emotionally affected by those letters that "simply relate the small events that punctuate the passage of time: roses picked at dusk, the laziness of a rainy Sunday, a child crying himself to sleep. Capturing the moment, these small slices of life, these small gusts of happiness, move me more deeply than all the rest." By surrounding himself with others with whom he can share feelings, Bauby can engage in emotional dialogues that "keep the vultures"—perhaps the bad feelings such as despair and anxiety that could so easily threaten to tear Bauby apart—"at bay."

Bauby is also aware of how his own actions toward others can be used in the service of adjusting his own inner state. "I try to compose features atrophied by paralysis into what I hope is a welcoming smile," he says. This kind of emotional engagement with others, even if the smile is "put on," practically guarantees a return smile from visitors that sends Bauby's mood soaring. Imagine instead the impact it might have on visitors if Bauby remained glum, his face immovable. Putting on a happy face, even at moments when he does not feel happy, ultimately allows Bauby to achieve the goal of effective self-modulation.

Finally, when the real people around him are not enough to create the inner illusion of an island of strength that Bauby needs, he conjures a relationship with a fantasy figure who is bigger, stronger, who can serve as a benign and encouraging caretaker, soothing his dark feelings away. When he notices a bust of Empress Eugenie, wife of Napoleon III and his hospital's patroness in a hallway, accompanied by a railwayman's account of her visit to the hospital years earlier, he escapes into the scene and imagines his relationship with Eugenie again and again.

> On one particularly windy day, I even dared to draw near and bury my face in the folds of her white gauzy dress with its broad satin stripes. It was as sweet as whipped cream, as cool as the morning dew. She did not send me away. She ran her fingers through my hair and said gently, "There, there, my child, you must be very patient," in a Spanish accent very like the neurologist's. She was no longer the empress of the French but a compassionate divinity in the manner of Saint Rita, patroness of lost causes.

In effect, Bauby has evoked the image of a comforting (m)other that he surely must have internalized in
early life, taken into the circuitry of his cortico-
limbic loops. In her imaginary arms, he derives the
comfort and encouragement that he needs to feel less
alone, to sustain hopefulness in the face of a situation
that would make many of us hopeless.

The richness of the relationship he conjures with
his imagined patroness and protector suggests early
life experiences with a mother with whom Bauby
could share his doubts about his shortcomings in a
positive atmosphere. For instance, when he notices
that the reflection of "the head of a man who seemed
to have emerged from a vat of formaldehyde" is himself, he feels a

> strange euphoria....Not only was I exiled, para-
> lyzed, mute, half deaf, deprived of all pleasures,
> and reduced to the existence of a jellyfish, but I
> was also horrible to behold. There comes a time
> when the heaping up of calamities brings on un-
> controllable nervous laughter—when, after a final
> blow from fate, we decide to treat it all as a joke.
> My jovial cackling at first disconcerted Eugenie,
> until she herself was infected by my mirth. We
> laughed until we cried. The municipal band then
> struck up a waltz and I was so merry that I would

willingly have risen and invited Eugenie to dance, had such a move been fitting. We would have whirled around miles of floor. Ever since then, whenever I go through the main hall, I detect a hint of amusement in the empress's smile.

Perhaps the image that best shows the inner island of strength that Bauby possesses in his dire situation, the result of positive experiences in early life with a powerful but benign and loving caretaker, is the symbolic meaning with which he invests the lighthouse just outside the hospital that lights up the rocky French coast. He describes it as

> tall, robust, and reassuring, in red and white stripes that reminded me of a rugby shirt....I placed myself at once under the protection of this brotherly symbol, guardian not just of sailors but of the sick—those castaways on the shores of loneliness. The lighthouse and I remain in constant touch, and I often call on it.

In the winter darkness, Bauby watches it "take up the torch, its hope-filled beams sweeping the horizon." In the shadow of its protection and its strength, Bauby says, "I am the greatest director of all time."

To become the directors of our own inner worlds requires that we be able to recognize what we are feeling and what is making us feel that way, that we then take the necessary steps to shift what we are feeling in a more comfortable direction when required, using all the tools at our disposal. But to make the adjustments of sensation and mind that can positively affect how we feel, we must first avoid being seduced into believing the perspective on ourselves, others, and the world around us that they tend to bring. We must both take our inner emotions very seriously, acknowledging their crucial role in shaping the world around us, and we must take them not so seriously as well, avoiding the pitfall of believing the perspective on the world—and the pessimism—that negative emotions all too often bring.

Notice that Bauby's tricks for creating the inner world that will keep him in this more comfortable mood state do not involve avoiding negative feelings. He struggles against sadness over his losses, shame at his state, anxiety about his helplessness, and anger at the seeming injustice of the situation. It is not the absence of these feelings but rather the fact that he has the skills to bring himself back from the brink of them that matters. He does not drown in them, because his emotional skills help him create an inner island of strength amid the storm of outer events and inner feelings that threaten to overwhelm him. It is not that his own private movie is always a comedy or full of Pollyannaish optimism that makes him a master illusionist, but rather that he is at the helm of his mind, his perspective, and his vision even as he has lost control of so much of the world around him, including his very own body. He is a master at directing where he will let himself go, ever attentive to the implications and inner impact of his choices. This means even allowing his emotions to take him to dark places when warranted. He knows that well-controlled anxiety or anger can act as a psychological fuel, the emotional equivalent of the liquid nitrogen and oxygen whose slow burn powers the space shuttle. As he puts it:

> To keep my mind sharp, to avoid descending into resigned indifference, I maintain a level of resentment and anger, neither too much nor too little, just as a pressure cooker has a safety valve to keep it from exploding.

It is observing, understanding, and ultimately knowing his mind and inner mood scape that make him the master illusionist that he is. Even when thrown into a new life where all the rules of his existence have been changed, and despite feeling at times that he is an exile with the existence of a jellyfish, Bauby's inner abilities allow him to remain in the driver's seat, in control of himself.

As Bauby acknowledges, attending to and modulating our own inner states is not always easy. "I can listen to the butterflies that flutter inside my head. To hear them, one must be calm and pay close attention, for their wingbeats are barely audible. Loud breathing is enough to drown them out." Altering our emotions to achieve a more optimistic stance requires conscious effort, at least initially, for people who struggle with difficult states of mind. Becoming more optimistic requires an active decision on our part that we will take charge to the greatest extent possible of how we are feeling and what is making us feel that way. It means that we will choose to change what we are thinking about or experiencing when it is not having the desired effect on our mood, that we will not take our mood as an inexorable given. And in return, with practice, our own sense of having an ability to remain comfortable inside and the sense of control of the world around us, which this ability ultimately brings, will grow. A whole inner island of psychological skills will coalesce under our feet, giving us a very real inner island on which to stand, even when the world around us threatens to make us feel at sea. With increased attention to his insides, Bauby notes, "This is astonishing: my hearing does not improve, yet I hear (the butterflies) better and better. I must have butterfly hearing."

Although Bauby died two days after his book was published in France, it went on to become an international bestseller. And what Bauby left behind is a record of his own struggles to sustain himself, pictures of a master illusionist in action, a story that allows us to study his techniques just as one might dissect the cinematic approaches of a master film director. In the process, Bauby left us a blueprint for how to enhance our own ability to hear his butterflies as well.

Chapter Nine

THE BEACON ON THE HORIZON, THE LIGHT WITHIN

AS I LAY IN BED that night, nine months pregnant during the hottest, driest July in New York history, I thought of Bauby. I was anticipating the birth of the baby daughter that I had wanted so much to have, and I was flooded by feelings of anxiety and elation and excitement all rolled into one. As I anticipated this new relationship, this new phase in my life beginning, I was also struggling with my feelings of sadness about another relationship. After over seven years of meeting four or five times a week, my analysis was ending. How would I weather the loss of the psychoanalyst that I was to stop seeing after tomorrow's session? I had been jarred awake by a dream that left me anxious and afraid, an image that had just woken me up from the already fitful sleep typical of late pregnancy. The dream was elegant if stark in its simplicity, an inner image handed to me on the eve of two momentous life events, like a message in a bottle from myself to me just waiting to be decoded. In the dream, I was standing on the terrace of my apartment, scanning the Manhattan skyline. With a start I realized that the Empire State Building, that fixture and beacon in the New York night, was no longer there. The terrain and topography of the city was no longer the same; a major landmark was missing. In reality, the Empire State Building had been something I could tell time by, peeking out my bedroom window when I woke up to see if its lights were out, suggesting it was after midnight. I could read the passage of the seasons in its lights as well, the red, white, and blue of the Fourth of July giving way to the eerie pumpkin orange floodlights that lit up Halloween night. In the dream, I felt lost and anxious, alone and unanchored, unable to get my bearings without the building's comforting light. Then I realized that the Empire State Building was not really gone after all. It was simply covered in a thick blanket of fog, a fog so dense that the building was temporarily blotted out, its light extinguished. I awoke with a start, anxious yet relieved to know that the building was still there. I got up and went out on the terrace to see whether, indeed, the building still stood in its usual location. Awake by now, I was sure, intellectually speaking, that it did. But still, to feel emotionally certain, I had to see for myself. I discovered that the fog was indeed thick outside, erasing the building from its usual place on the horizon, obscuring its beacon of light. Yet I found I could picture it anyway. I could see it, project a picture of it back into the skyline even though it was invisible to me at the moment. The ability to conjure the building in my imagination despite the fog was within me because a vision within me of the building was present. But difficult inner emotions like anxiety—which I believe the fog represented in the dream—could certainly make the task of seeing it much more difficult.

In this book, I have argued that our emotions serve as the fog that clouds our perspective on ourselves and the future or as the bright skies that help us illuminate and clarify our place in the world. And I have asserted that our ability to modulate our own inner states of mind ultimately determines whether we see the glass as half empty or half full. In addition, I have argued that there is a reciprocal interaction between our emotional state and our sense that we exert control over the world around us. Sustaining healthy illusion that we are more in the driver's seat than we really are is the primary way to become more optimistic. In contrast, the often more "realistic" perceptions of those who are anxious and depressed make the world a place in which we feel a complete lack of control, a perspective that sends us sinking into existential despair. I have suggested that the capacity for self-regulation that we learn through interactions with important caretakers in early life is what determines how effectively we modulate emotions later on. These lessons about ourselves and others and the moods that permeate the interactions of our first three years are literally etched into the neural circuitry of the brain through the formation of cortico-limbic loops. It is this neural circuitry that determines in large measure whether our perspective is primarily one of optimism or pessimism in adulthood, affecting whether we spend much of our time in dysregulated states struggling with problematic emotions or most of our moments feeling in the driver's seat of our self. Because of the manner in which our neural circuitry evolves in the context of early life relationships, our ability to modulate our own inner states is always connected to our perspectives on self and other, to our understanding of the rules that make relationships work. Our inner emotional life is inextricably peopled. There are people from our past attached to every emotion we have. And when we lack the capacity to regulate ourselves effectively, we are often left struggling with negative views of our self long into adulthood, views that make us overly reliant on eliciting certain reactions from people in the world around us. Thus, our capacity for self-modulation and our sense of autonomy are linked as well.

Yet despite the long-lasting impact of early life experience on the cortico-limbic reins that serve as the basis for self-control in later life, there are ways to improve up our capacity for mood modulation. We have seen how putting on a happy face and changing how we think about what happens to us can help to change our mood and give us a much needed sense of self-control. An optimistic explanatory style or the use of downward comparisons with others can bolster our mood as well as our sense of self. And if making our existing cortico-limbic loops function differently isn't enough, psychotherapy and the new experience of a relationship that it provides can literally help us rewire the brain circuitry laid down in early life. With a solid capacity for mood modulation, we can face even the most difficult aspects of life with a sense of inner autonomy, not only maximizing how well we feel but also literally changing how many options we have and how we will fare in the world.

Optimism depends upon having the most secure and certain beacon within us possible. This inner island of self-control, sense of goodness, and self-confidence is either acquired easily through our early life experiences with caretakers or arrived at later in life with more effort, in my case through psycho-analysis. Bauby's lighthouse and my Empire State Building are the symbolic representatives of the good enough caretakers who nurtured us through good moods and bad, accepted our feelings, and slowly showed us how to manage our inner states more ef-fectively for ourselves. Having taken in important as-pects of the people who, through these interactions, taught us to modulate our inner states for ourselves, one major task of development is to slowly integrate the beacons around us instead. We must incorporate and internalize them to help us form the solid island of self-control that keeps us in good stead even when we are without them. Our sense of being all right even in the dead of night when the world around us is cloaked in fog depends, in turn, on our ability to use that inner light to cut through foggy emotions like sadness, shame, and anxiety. We must project that core of strength outward, onto the horizon, to make it manifest in the world around us. The ability to throw this internalized aspect of the good self back out into the world in turn provides the illusion of an island on the horizon that signals safe harbor, a beacon by which to steer our course when we most need it.

But no man is an island. We need an early caretaker or a later-life relationship that nurtures us to form the inner representation of the lighthouse whose light lives on within us. We also need to be able to detach ourselves from this original source of light, whether it comes from our early life caretakers or the cortico-limbic mechanics whose assistance we seek in later life. Internalizing what was once outside of ourselves is ultimately the only way to become autonomous and independent. The alternative is remaining dependent on others in problematic ways to avoid being plunged into the darkness with which our failed ability to modulate our inner states threatens us. Like a performer who jumps through hoops in an attempt to get the spotlight to follow us, we are left trying to control the uncontrollable in our quest to bask in the light of positive feelings and the sense of security that we cannot generate for ourselves. And, as I mused that night after my dream, possessing this lighthouse within becomes essential as we enter parenthood, seeking to shape the cortico-limbic loops of our tiny charges in a way that promotes mastery of inner feelings and states of mind. The transfer of this inner beacon from parent to child, mother to daughter, generation to generation, as the Olympic flame is passed from one torchbearer to the next, is the true task of parenting.

This focus on how we acquire and maintain this beacon within is a new one in psychology. There's a new movement afoot called positive psychology which suggests that we should study desirable human states like happiness, optimism, and resilience as extensively as we study pathological ones like depression. This idea is just now beginning to garner the attention and funding that it deserves. Already investigations that focus on the positive are beginning to bear fruit. In his ground-breaking book *Emotional Intelligence,* Daniel Goleman concluded that our capacity for autonomous emotional regulation is crucial.[1] Becoming a masterful mood modulator like Bauby is probably worthwhile simply because it makes us feel better more of the time. But Goleman also suggested that there are probably many other important consequences of having or not having these inner emotional skills. For instance, maximal productivity and progress toward your goals depends upon your ability to tolerate frustration, control your impulses, and delay gratification. Emotions tend instead to push us in the direction of taking action. Indeed, the fact that they ready us for action, as when fear sends blood pumping through our leg muscles, is one of their uses, probably one of the reasons that they evolved. Yet restraining yourself from simply acting on feelings—such as blowing up at the sales clerk who is trying to help you—depends in turn on being able to tolerate and modulate negative feeling states, such as frustration and anger, to keep them inside and work with them instead of simply letting them fly.

Goleman's conclusions are supported by the work of David Myers and Ed Diener on happiness. In answer to the question of who is happy, they conclude from a flood of recent studies on subjective well-being that frequent positive affects and infrequent negative affects—in other words, effective emotion self-modulation—are key. Their work also reveals that variables such as age, gender, race, and socioeconomic class do not predict happiness; luckily, the capacity for optimism and the sense of happiness that accompanies it are equal-opportunity variables.[2]

In addition, with the capacity for mood modulation in place, the stage is set for creativity and fulfillment, for living life in the state that Mihaly Csikszentmihalyi calls "flow."[3] Another useful product of the new positive psychology movement, his work demonstrates that flow states are inherently reinforcing psychological states in which we perform at our best, enjoy ourselves most, and engage in the task at hand with a sense of meaning and purpose. They are the states in which athletes describe feeling as if they are moving fluidly and effortlessly, a psychological experience that is indeed accompanied by a decrease in and a streamlining of brain activity. It is as if we are psychologically and biologically trimmed to an efficient inner core that operates with no excess spinning of our wheels. The fact that the brain's activity quiets during flow, as if the brain is working in its most effective manner, suggests that we are using well-rehearsed circuits that are maximally efficient. As Csikszentmihalyi notes, flow is most likely to occur when we are in the zone between boredom and anxiety. In other words, we enjoy a tennis game more when our opponent is evenly matched, when we are neither bored by their lack of skill nor made anxious by their superiority. But if flow depends on entering the emotional zone between boredom and anxiety, then possessing superior mood modulatory capabilities will ensure that we enter more frequently the feeling space that is a prerequisite for flow. Since Csikszentmihalyi's research indicates that people who spend more time in flow rate themselves as happier and more optimistic, our conclusions are the same: the capacity for mood modulation underlies the ability to sustain an optimistic stance. It is the nagging tug of anxiety, depression, and chronic anger that keeps us out of the mood states required to enter flow, and it is our inability to pull ourselves out of these same states that are also responsible for making us unhappy and pessimistic.

Another topic that our new interest in positive psychology places front and center is the subject of what makes us resilient in the face of childhood adversity. What is it that enables us to play a poor hand well?[4] When we focus on what we know about the answer to this question, one finding seems to stand out. What seems to make much of the difference for many of those who turned out well despite abuse and neglect at the hands of others was the presence of one adult—a teacher, a neighbor, a relative, a priest— who took an interest. In other words, in keeping with my assertion that optimism's circuitry is shaped in the crucible of intensive early life interactions with a primary caretaker, it makes sense that all it might take to pass the torch from one generation to the next is one well-timed flame bearer. But the explosive emotions and the loss of self-control that are currently apparent everywhere—from Jerry Springer to Columbine high school—suggest that all too often that one much-needed person is simply nowhere to be seen.

From emotional intelligence and flow, to resiliency, positive psychology promises to show us the uniting forces that underlie mental health, and in so doing perhaps give us an edge in understanding what can go wrong. Even a phenomenon such as the placebo effect—in which one person gives another the ability to conjure an island of hope on the horizon—represents a temporary transfer of optimism, a lending of a light at the end of the tunnel to someone who is currently plunged in hopeless darkness. Investigation in scientific terms of how such phenomena work between people to prevent demoralization is just beginning. If there were a new drug as powerful in its effect as placebos can be, it would be front page news. It's about time that we started trying to understand the mechanism of action that allows hope to be taken in, even if only temporarily, by the hopeless.[5]

As researchers begin to recognize that an individual's capacity for mood modulation, learned in early childhood, can make all the difference in how his life is experienced, we also have growing evidence of dys-regulation all around us in the form of mad shooting sprees, skyrocketing rates of anxiety and depression in the young, and the breakdown of some of the same relationships that I am asserting are so crucial in forming our cortico-limbic loops in the first place.

In addition to the high social costs of such dys-regulation, there is also the human cost, the fact that a failure of the early life relationships that should produce mood modulation and positive self-esteem leaves us mired in misery long into adulthood. On a person-to-person basis as an analyst, hearing the childhood stories and later life experiences of those who lack the capacity to enjoy positive states of be-ing, such as elation, and who cannot control negative states of mind, such as anger, shame, and despair, is simply downright painful. One patient of mine told the story of how his grandmother, who raised him, treated his new puppy. She was so harsh in house-breaking the dog that in the process of "teaching" him she actually ended up breaking his spirit instead. In the face of such an environment, the dog soon stopped eating and seemed anxious even being in the same room with my patient's grandmother. This anx-iety and skittishness seemed to contribute to the dog's failure to learn, to accidents, such as urinating on the rug, that in turn elicited more wrath, harsher treatments. The puppy soon stopped eating and died. A vet might have called it "failure to thrive," but the result of this kind of abuse in children has also been called "soul murder." Although my patient's own soul was not dead, it was damaged by the treatment he received in early life at the hands of his grandmother. He too had a kind of emotional failure to thrive rooted in these experiences that persisted into adulthood. He lacked the capacity for excited elation and spontaneity, often feeling empty and bland instead. And he kept expecting a bombshell around the next corner when things went well anyway. What story did he find himself preoccupied with in adulthood? The tale of the Donner party, a group of pioneers who attempted to cross a mountain pass just as winter set in, getting stranded and snowed in and gradually starving to death. The patient vividly described what he imagined about the situation, picturing a settler looking up at the snow and praying for it to stop. As the snow continued and continued and the gravity of the situation set in, he envisioned the settler slowly reaching the conclusion that all his prayers were for naught, that he was living in a godless universe in which none of his desires or wishes or attempts to rescue himself from the situation could make a difference. The continuing snowfall was evidence of how indifferent the universe was to his plight or perhaps even nature's way of being downright cruel.

In hearing the story in its various incarnations over several years of therapy, I came to see the snow as a symbol of the cold, harsh feelings showered on the patient by his grandmother, a kind of metaphor for the climate that made his puppy give up and go under. I also came to realize that one of the patient's emotional responses to his upbringing had been to become emotionally frozen, icy himself. He had handled the intensity of his grandmother's harsh upbringing by avoiding intense feelings altogether. But this style of emotional coping had affected everything in his life. He lacked joie de vivre in his work and relationships, and his sense of self was plagued by doubt and self-criticism, the same doubt and self-criticism that he expected others to heap upon him. He described feeling frozen much of the time, and he frequently seemed that way with me as well. On the few occasions when he did break into tears, I came to appreciate that the frozenness was an alternative to drowning, being emotionally flooded. On the occasions when he did cry, he was wracked by paroxysms of sobs and literally wrapped his own arms around himself, as if to embrace himself in a semblance of a hug for comfort. For him there was no guarantee of a loving and benevolent caretaker being available in his hour of need.

In short, my patient's early life experiences contributed to his sense that there was no beacon, no lighthouse on the horizon, and no light that lived within, either. No wonder he felt a kind of existential despair and lack of meaning that was in fact deeply rooted in his experience of his inner self as empty. But after many discussions of the themes of the Donner Pass story in the setting of what I hoped was a warm and accepting relationship with me, the patient pointed out one crucial but until then omitted fact about the story: several children had survived and were discovered the next spring. It wasn't much to go on, perhaps, but it did represent a sliver of hope on the horizon, the possibility of rescue.

The fact remains that almost all of us struggle with moods and their modulation. Recent research shows that the limbic system has a kind of trip wire, a pathway that allows it to escape cortical control when it is stoked up enough about something. In contrast to what we used to think, its very anatomy means that Aristotle and Descartes were wrong and that the cortex and the thinking it produces, as impressive as it is, cannot be counted on to control our emotions completely.[6] These new findings mean that the modulation of our inner mood states is something that is not a given for anyone, something that is part of the human condition with which we have to struggle.

Another benefit of the positive psychology movement is that by understanding positive states of being like the in-control stance of optimists, we may also better comprehend both what interferes with mental health and well-being and how to make problematic perspectives like pessimism better. For instance, when Martin Seligman began to shift his focus to an understanding of the protective thought patterns of optimists and their positive explanatory styles, he began to understand how to push pessimists in a more healthy direction by teaching them to think differently. In addition, understanding the mechanisms underlying positive states of being also enabled him to look for ways to make children more resilient, to immunize them against despair. Developing these kinds of strategies allows us to reach for that holy grail of mental health—prevention.[7]

At the same time that the positive psychology movement is gathering steam, shifting the focus of what we study, neuroscience continues to advance at a rapid pace, raising the intriguing possibility that the two can be combined, allowing us to understand the brain mechanisms of positive states of mind such as happiness. Already Richard Davidson and colleagues are mapping the brain areas responsible for positive emotions and looking at how thinking in various ways affects the brain.[8] Neurologist Antonio Damasio and colleagues have begun to study the neurophysiology behind emotional mastery, suggesting that certain individuals can indeed achieve masterful mood modulation through practice. For instance, when the pianist Maria Joao Pires asserted that she could either reduce or allow the flow of emotion to her body, Damasio and his wife, Hanna, also a neuroscientist, originally thought this was an artist's romantic but inaccurate notion. Yet when they hooked her up to a complex psychophysiological apparatus while she listened to two short pieces of music either allowing or inhibiting her emotions, they learned that she was indeed correct. She was able to alter her own inner state in a way that was reflected in such basic bodily processes as heart rate, skin conductance, and facial movement.[9] A positive psychological perspective combined with advances in neuroscience may allow us to understand the masterful mood modulation that underlies the performances of great artists—the musicians, actors, and dancers for whom mood modulation is stock-in-trade. Advances in neuroscience may also further clarify how it is that later life experiences such as intensive psychotherapy can literally allow us to rewire the circuitry itself, giving us the chance to learn to modulate our own inner states more effectively.

Furthermore, in addition to using positive psychology to enable us to understand what allows individuals to modulate feelings effectively for themselves, studying healthy individuals allows us to better understand the ways in which emotions are expressed and handled within relationships that succeed. What makes people feel good and comfortable with each other and enables the bonds they forge to endure? The work of John Gottman, which looks at both marriages that succeed and those that don't, has demonstrated that a certain type of getting in step with each other is reflected in the neurophysiological profiles of spouses whose marriages are happy. Through their interactions, they foster the effectiveness of each of their individual capacities to regulate their inner states rather than the derailment of positive emotional states more typical of marriages that fail.[10]

As I reflect on the way in which my own lengthy

psychoanalytic experience has enabled me to more effectively sustain the illusion of an island, I realize that it seems to have gradually shifted my sense of my ability to autonomously regulate my inner states for myself in a more positive direction. Probably this happened gradually, over time, by exploring and exposing my feelings and fantasies, good and bad, in the context of a relationship in which the ruptures, real and imagined, produced by negative feelings were always talked about and repaired. The taking in of this relationship—the caretaker who remained warm and accepting, interested in understanding, and personally accessible even in the face of my revelations of my most negative self—was like taking in the strong and steady Empire State Building, the light that I could tell time by and that defined and shaped the skyline around me. Once this beacon was firmly established within me, I became more able to throw its light out into the world to make it seem a warmer place as well, much as a ventriloquist can throw his voice to animate an otherwise lifeless doll. Over time I stopped relying on the relationship with my analyst and my analyst himself to provide the light, and gradually shifted from peninsula to island myself. And because I no longer relied on the real Empire State Building but on my inner image of it, I could conjure its presence even when it was no longer really there, even in moments where fog obscured it. I was perched between two moments in time, about to belatedly leave behind childhood and the new emotional home—and parent—that had been so important to me for seven years. I was awaiting the arrival of someone I had long anticipated but didn't yet know, someone whose story was waiting to be written, whose cortico-limbic loops would be shaped by me through the simple yet profound act of being Mom. I saw that as I had become a more effective modulator of my own inner states, a very real kind of psychological ground had coalesced under my feet as well, giving me an internal island of strength from which to operate. I now had a way to create my own illusion of an island, my own lighthouse on the horizon that could guide me and give me a landmark to swim for when the going got tough. With this newly garnered ability, I was ready to face whatever lay ahead with a more optimistic outlook. Of course I knew I would miss my almost daily meetings with the Empire State Building himself, just as I would miss the New York skyline if I moved away. But my dream ultimately reassured me that he would endure within my inner landscape for years to come, helping me to generate a light within that would guide me through future fogs. The legacy of his importance in my life would enable me to better pass the torch along to the patients I treat as well. And to the beautiful little girl with the innocent and inquisitive blue eyes and the engaging toothless grin who now lies beside me dreaming of butterflies, islands, and lighthouses beckoning to her in the night.

Notes

Chapter One

1. Though drawn from a study examining spatial memory in rats (Morris, R.G.M. (1981). Spatial localization does not require the presence of local cues. *Learning and Motivation, 12,* 239–260.), this study effectively comments on the links between early experience, the expectations it creates (which might be termed hope or despair) and persistence in searching for an island that one cannot even see. For a more thorough review of related studies that also bear upon these issues, see Brandeis, R., Brandys, Y., and Yehuda, S. (1989). The use of the Morris Water Maze in the study of memory and learning. *International Journal of Neuroscience, 48,* 29–69.

2. For a review of the phenomenon of depressive realism, see Alloy, L. B., & Abramson, L. Y. (1988). Depressive realism: Four theoretical perspectives. In L. B. Alloy (ed.), *Cognitive processes in depression.* New York: Guilford Press.

3. Frankl, V. E. (1959). *Man's search for meaning.* New York: Simon & Schuster. Originally titled *From*

death-camp to existentialism, this book details the
psychiatrist's experiences in Auschwitz and his first-
hand observations about the anatomy of hope and
despair. In addition, it introduces logotherapy, a
psychotherapeutic theory derived from Frankl's experiences in which the job of the therapist is to help
his patient uncover meaning in all of his experiences, including the experience of suffering.

4. See Seligman, M. (1990). *Learned optimism.* New
York: Pocket Books. Psychologist Martin Seligman
studied the thought patterns of people who persevere and succeed, from star swimmers to insurance
salesmen, from basketball players to politicians, using his method content analysis of verbatim expla-
nations (CAVE), which analyzes how these people
tend to explain positive and negative events.
Learned optimism includes a chapter about the
health effects of optimism and pessimism.

5. See Visintainer, J., Volpicelli, J., & Seligman, M.
(1982). Tumor rejection in rats after inescapable or
escapable shock. *Science, 216,* 437–439.

6. See Vaillant, G. (1995). *Adaptation to life* (rev. ed.).
Cambridge, MA: Harvard University Press. George
Vaillant's article summarizes the results of the Grant
study of two hundred Harvard undergraduates se-
lected in 1939–1944 and followed prospectively for
over fifty years on a variety of psychological and
health measures.

Chapter Two

1. See Bowers, G. (1981). Mood and memory. *American Psychologist, 36,* 129–148, for a collection of Bower's seminal findings.
2. See Schachter, D. L. (ed.). et al. (Coyle, J. T., Fischbach, G. D., Mesulam, M. M., and Sullivan, L. E.) (1995). *Memory distortions: How minds, brains and societies reconstruct the past.* Cambridge, MA: Harvard University Press. This book reviews the mood-congruence literature, including a chapter entitled "Mood congruent memory biases in anxiety and depression." Mineka, S. and Nugent, K.
3. See Eich, E., Macaulay, D., & Lam, R. W. (1997). Mania, depression, and mood-dependent memory. *Cognition and Emotion, 11,* 607–618. Although mood-congruence research is often conducted on "normals," this study examined mood congruence in naturally rapidly cycling patients with bipolar disorder or manic depression.
4. See Mayer, J. D., McCormick, L. J., & Strong, S. E. (1995). Mood-congruent memory and natural mood: New evidence. *Personality and Social Psychology Bulletin, 21,* 736–746. Unlike many mood-congruence studies, this one focuses on naturally occurring rather than experimentally induced emotions.
5. For more details, see Jamison, K. R. (1995). *An unquiet mind.* New York: Knopf.

6. Dewberry, C., & Richardson, S. (1990). The effect of anxiety on optimism. *Journal of Social Psychology,* *130,* 731–738.

Chapter Three

1. This phenomenon was originally discovered by Ellen Langer at Harvard University, who dubbed it the *illusion of control* and studied its occurrence in her subjects' thinking about probabilistic phenomena, such as coin tosses. See also Langer, E. J. (1975). The illusion of control. *Journal of Personality and Social Psychology,* *32,* 311–328; Langer, E. J., & Roth, J. (1975). Heads I win, tails it's chance: The illusion of control as a function of the sequence of outcomes in a purely chance task. *Journal of Personality and Social Psychology,* *32,* 951–955.

2. See Fleming, J. H., & Darley, J. M. (1990). The purposeful action sequence and the "illusion of control." *Personality and Social Psychology Bulletin, 16,* 346–357.

3. Biner, P. M., Angle, S. T., Park, J. H., Mellinger, A. E., et al. (1995). Need state and the illusion of control. *Personality and Social Psychology Bulletin, 21,* 899–907.

4. Alloy, L. B., & Clements, C. M. (1992). Illusion of control: Invulnerability to negative affect and depressive symptoms after laboratory and natural stressors. *Journal of Social Psychology, 101,* 234–245.

5. Dewberry, C., Ing, M., James, S., & Nixon, M. (1990). Anxiety and unrealistic optimism. *Journal of Abnormal Psychology, 101,* 234–245.
6. Sanderson, W. C., Rapee, R. M., & Barlow, D. H. (1989). The influence of an illusion of control on panic attacks induced via inhalation of 5.5% carbon dioxide-enriched air. *Archives of General Psychiatry, 46,* 157–162.
7. Taylor, S. E., & Brown, J. D. (1988). Illusion and well-being: A social psychological perspective on mental health. *Psychological Bulletin, 103,* 193–210.
8. Taylor, S. E., & Armor, D. A. (1996). Positive illusion and coping with adversity. *Journal of Personality, 64,* 873–898. See also Taylor, S. E. (1989). *Positive illusions: Creative self-deception and the healthy mind.* New York: Basic Books. Taylor has also argued that the illusion of control is an effective means of affect regulation.
9. See Drake, R. A. (1984). Lateral asymmetry of personal optimism. *Journal of Research in Personality, 18,* 497–507; see also Johnson, E. I., & Tversky, A. (1983). Affect, generalization and the perception of risk. *Journal of Personality and Social Psychology, 45,* 20–31.
10. Larson, R. (1989). Is feeling in control related to happiness in daily life? *Psychological Reports, 64,* 775–784.
11. Seligman, M. E. (1990). *Learned optimism.* New York: Pocket Books.

12. Brown, G. E., & Stroup, K. (1988). Learned help-lessness in the cockroach (*Periplaneta americana*). *Behavioral and Neural Biology, 50,* 246–250.

13. Breier, A., Albus, M., Pickar, D., & Zahn, T. P. (1987). Controllable and uncontrollable stress in humans: Alterations in mood and neuroendocrine and psychophysiological function. *American Journal of Psychiatry, 144,* 1419–1425.

14. Lewis, M., Alessandri, S. M., & Sullivan, M. W. (1990). Violation of expectancy, loss of control and anger expressions in young infants. *Developmental Psychology, 26,* 745–751.

Chapter Four

1. See Hofer's chapter on caretakers as brain trainers in Roose, S. P., & Glick, R. A. (1995). *Anxiety as symptom and signal.* Hillsdale, NJ: Analytic Press.

2. Damasio, A. R. (1994). *Descartes' error: Emotion, reason, and the human brain.* New York: Putnam.

3. See Schore, A. (1994). *Affect regulation and the origins of the self: The neurobiology of emotional development.* Hillsdale, NJ: Lawrence Erlbaum. The "dual component orbitofrontal system" of affect regulation outlined in this chapter, consisting of two cortico-limbic loops formed in the first and second year of life, respectively, is the theoretical synthesis of Allan Schore. His study is an important integra-

tion of neurobiological detail, development, and psychoanalytic theory.

4. For a succinct summary of this work, see Beebe, A., Lachmann, F., & Jaffee, J. (1997). Mother–infant interaction structures and presymbolic self- and object-representations. *Psychoanalytic Dialogues, 7,* 133–187.

5. Again, this synthesis of neurobiology and development is the work of Allan Schore (see footnote 3).

6. Tulkin, S. R., & Kagan, J. (1972). Mother–infant interaction in the first year of life. *Child Development, 43,* 31–42.

7. For a discussion of the evolution of representations and the differences in implicit and explicit memory, see my earlier work, Vaughan, S. C. (1997). *The talking cure: The science behind psychotherapy.* New York: Putnam.

8. Stern, D. (1985). *The interpersonal world of the infant.* New York: Basic Books.

9. Beebe, B., & Lachmann, F. M. (1994). Representation and internalization in infancy: Three principles of salience. *Psychoanalytic Psychology, 11,* 127–165.

10. Power, M. J., & Chapieski, M. L. (1986). Childrearing and impulse control in toddlers: A naturalistic investigation. *Developmental Psychology, 22,* 271–275.

11. The consequences of misattunement, both psychological and biological, are outlined in Schore (1994) (see footnote 3). He sees these interactions in early

relationships as crucial to the development of the
second cortico-limbic loop.

12. Dunn, J., Brown, J., & Beardsall, L. (1991). Family
talk about feeling states and children's later understanding of others' emotions. *Developmental
Psychology, 27,* 448–455.

13. Cicchetti, D., Ganiban, J., & Barnett, D. (1991).
Contributions from the study of high-risk popula-
tions to understanding the development of emotion
regulation. In Garber, J., & Dodge, K. A. (eds.),
*The development of emotion regulation and dysregula-
tion* (pp. 15–48). New York: Cambridge University
Press.

14. Bishop, S. J., & Rothbaum, F. (1992). Parents' ac-
ceptance of control needs and preschoolers' social
behaviour: A longitudinal study. *Canadian Journal
of Behavioural Science, 24,* 171–185.

15. Kagan, J. (1994). *Galen's Prophecy: Temperament in
human nature.* New York: Basic Books.

16. Davidson, R. (1994). Asymmetric brain function,
affective style and psychopathology: The role of
early experience and plasticity. *Development and
Psychopathology, 6,* 741–758.

Chapter Five

1. Kernberg, O. F. (1982). Self, ego, affects, and
drives. *Journal of the American Psychoanalytic
Association, 30,* 893–917.

2. Luborsky, L., & Crits-Christoph, P. (1990). *Understanding transference: The CCRT method.* New York: Basic Books.

3. For more about the process of building relationship models, including the interplay of fantasy and historical events, see chapters 4–7 of Vaughan, S. C. (1997). *The talking cure: The science behind psychotherapy.* New York: Putnam.

4. For an excellent overview of the current state of research on all aspects of emotions, see Oatley, K., & Jenkins, J. M. (1996). *Understanding emotion.* Cambridge, MA: Blackwell Publishers.

5. Spangler, G., & Grossman, K. E. (1993). Biobehavioral organization in securely and insecurely attached infants. *Child Development, 64,* 1439–1450.

6. Waters, E., Merrick, S. K., Albersheim, L. J., & Tribous, D. (1995). *Attachment security from infancy to adulthood: A 20-year longitudinal study of attachment security in infancy and early adulthood.* Paper presented to the Biennial Meeting of the Society for Research on Child Development, Indianapolis, IN.

7. George, C., Kaplan, N., & Main, M. (1985). *The Berkeley Adult Attachment Inventory.* Unpublished protocol, Department of Psychology, University of California, Berkeley.

8. The specific study is found in Fonagy, P., Steele, H., & Steele, M. (1991). Maternal representations of attachment during pregnancy predict the organization of infant–mother attachment at one year of

age. *Child Development, 62,* 891–905. See also
Fonagy, P., Steele, M., Moran, G. S., Steele, M., &
Higgitt, A. C. (1993). Measuring the ghost in the
nursery: An empirical study of the relations between
parents' mental representations of childhood experiences and their infants' security of attachment.
Journal of the American Psychoanalytic Association,
41, 957–989.

9. Vaughn, B., Egeland, B., Sroufe, L. A., & Waters,
E. (1979). Individual differences in infant–mother
attachment at twelve and eighteen months:
Stability and change in families under stress. *Child
Development, 59,* 971–975.

10. Goldberg, S., MacKay, S., & Rochester, M. (1994).
Affect, attachment and maternal responsiveness.
Infant Behavior and Development, 17, 335–339.

Chapter Seven

1. Vaughan, S. C., Marshall, R. D., Vaughan, R., et al.
Can we do psychoanalytic outcome research?: A fea-
sibility study. *Journal of the American Psychoanalytic
Association,* in press.

2. For a discussion of historical perspectives on emo-
tion, see Oatley, K., & Jenkins, J. M. (1996).
Understanding emotion. Cambridge, MA: Blackwell
Publishers.

3. Seligman, M. (1990). *Learned optimism.* New York:
Pocket Books.

4. Aspinwall, L. G., & Taylor, S. E. (1993). Effects of social comparison direction, threat, and self-esteem on affect, self-evaluation, and expected success. *Journal of Personality and Social Psychology, 64,* 708–722.
5. As cited in His Holiness the Dalai Lama, & Cutler, H. C. (1999). *The art of happiness: A handbook for living.* New York: Riverhead Books.
6. VanderZee, K. I., Buunk, B. P., DeRuiter, J. H., Templelaar, R., et al. (1996). Social comparison and the subjective well-being of cancer patients. *Basic and Applied Social Psychology, 18,* 453–468.
7. Swallow, S. R., & Kuiper, N. A. (1993). Social comparison in dysphoria and nondysphoria: Differences in target similarity and specificity. *Cognitive Therapy and Research, 17,* 103–122.
8. Wills, T. A. (1981). Downward comparisons principles in social psychology. *Psychological Bulletin, 90,* 245–271.
9. His Holiness the Dalai Lama, & Cutler, H. C. (1999). *The art of happiness: A handbook for living.* New York: Riverhead Books.
10. Zajonc, R. B., Murphy, S. T., & Inglehart, M. (1989). Feeling and facial efference: Implications of the vascular theory of emotion. *Psychological Review, 96,* 395–416.
11. Strack, F., Martin, L. L., & Stepper, S. (1988). Inhibiting and facilitating conditions of the human smile: A non-obtrusive test of the facial feedback

hypothesis. *Journal of Personality and Social Psychology, 54,* 768–777.

12. Carpenter, P. J. (1992). Perceived control as a predictor of distress in children undergoing invasive medical procedures. *Journal of Pediatric Psychology, 17,* 757–773.

13. Stratton, V. N., & Zalanowski, A. H. (1997). The relationship between characteristic moods and most commonly listened to types of music. *Journal of Music Therapy, 34,* 129–140.

14. Vaughan, S. C. (1997). *The talking cure: The science behind psychotherapy.* New York: Putnam.

15. Luborsky, L., & Crits-Christoph, P. (1990). *Understanding transference: The Core Conflictual Relationship Theme method* (2nd ed.). Washington, DC: American Psychological Associate.

16. Vaughan, S. C. (1997). *The talking cure: The science behind psychotherapy.* New York: Putnam.

17. Orlinsky, D. E., & Geller, J. D. (1993). Patients' representations of their therapists and therapy: New measures. In Miller, N. E., Luborsky, L., et al. (eds.), *Psychodynamic treatment research: A handbook for clinical practice* (pp. 423–466). New York: Basic Books.

Chapter Eight

1. Bauby, J. D. (1997). *The diving-bell and the butterfly.* New York: Knopf.

2. Neurologist Antonio Damasio has argued (Damasio, A. (1999). *The feeling of what happens: Body and emotion in the making of consciousness.* San Diego, CA: Harcourt, Inc.) that the severed feedback from Bauby's paralyzed body might tend to limit the intensity of the emotional reactions that Bauby experiences. However, my own experiences consulting on two suicidal patients with locked in syndrome suggest that it is indeed possible to have intense feelings despite the severed feedback from the body present in the disorder.

Chapter Nine

1. Goleman, D. (1995). *Emotional intelligence: Why it can matter more than IQ.* New York: Bantam Books.
2. Myers, D. G., & Diener, E. (1995). Who is happy? *Psychological Science, 6,* 10–19.
3. Csikszenthihalyi, M. (1990). *Flow: The psychology of optimal experience.* New York: Harper and Row.
4. Katz, M. (1997). *On playing a poor hand well: Insights from the lives of those who have overcome childhood risks and adversities.* New York: W.W. Norton.
5. Brody, H. (1997). The doctor as therapeutic agent: A placebo effect research agenda. In A. Harrington et al. (eds.), *The placebo effect: An interdisciplinary exploration* (pp. 77–92). Cambridge, MA: Harvard University Press.

6. LeDoux, J. (1996). *The emotional brain: The mysterious underpinnings of emotional life.* New York: Simon and Schuster.
7. Seligman, M. (1995). *The optimistic child.* New York: Harper Collins.
8. Lane, R. D., Reiman, E. M., Ahem, G. L., Schwartz, G. E., & Davidson, R. J. (1997). Neuroanatomical correlates of happiness, sadness and disgust. *American Journal of Psychiatry, 154,* 926–933.
9. Damasio, A. (1999). *The feeling of what happens: Body and emotion in the making of consciousness.* San Diego, CA: Harcourt, Inc.
10. Gottman, J. (1993). *What predicts divorce: The relationship between marital processes and marital outcomes.* Hillsdale, NJ: Lawrence Erlbaum.

Index

action
  emotions and, 205
  vs. inaction, 46–47
aggression, 98, 99, 101–4, 106
AIDS, perceived risk of, 45
alexithymia, 90–91
altruistic behavior, 160
amygdala, 65–67
  and self-regulation, 63–64
anger, 106, 108, 116, 136, 158
  repressed and suppressed,
    100, 104, 110
  in therapist, 100, 130, 140
antidepressants, 19, 105, 146–
    48
anxiety, 36–37, 41, 58, 149–
    50
  and action vs. inaction, 47
  breaking out of spiral of,
    41–42
  See also threats and dangers;
    worrying
anxiety disorders, 146–48
  See also panic attacks
attachment styles, 118–19
  avoidant, 115, 117
  resistant/ambivalent, 116,
    117

secure, 116–19, 169
attack. *See* aggression
attributional style, 43, 153–
    60, 213
autonomy, 93, 100, 118, 120,
    121
  benefits of having achieved,
    34, 57, 173
  inner sense of, 34, 57–59
  psychotherapy as enhancing,
    170
  and self-regulation, 126–27,
    170–71, 201–2
  See also independence; self-
    control

Bauby, Jean-Dominique, 173–
    96, 202, 231*n*2
Beebe, Beatrice, 78–81
behavior that induces opti-
    mism, 160–63
beliefs. *See* cognitions
betrayal and retribution, 99–
    100, 106
bipolar disorder, 18–19, 21,
    31–32
  See also mood disorders
birth control, use of, 47

emotional failure to thrive, 209–12
emotional indifference, 107–9, 114–15
Emotional Intelligence (Goleman), 204–5
emotions
  ability to go through different, 23, 30–32
  acting on, 205
  conscious effort to alter, 195
  as contagious, 164
  difficulty expressing, 114, 115
  impact, 16–21
  language and, 89–91
  purposes, 164
  and relations with other people, 73–74
  See also mood(s); self-regulation; *specific topics*
empathy, development of, 90
emptiness, feeling of, 126, 129, 143, 153, 212
envy, 140, 158
exhibitionistic behavior, 102–3
existential despair, 212
explanatory style. *See* attributional style

failure, response to, 153–54
failure to thrive, 209–12
faith. *See* illusion, of an island
fantasy(ies), 112, 113, 180, 183–84, 187

feelings. *See* emotions
flow, 206–7
Frankl, Viktor E., 7, 219n3
Freud, Sigmund, 151, 165–66
fusion and merger, 103–5

gamblers, 47
Goleman, Daniel, 204–5
Gottman, John, 215
guilt, 98, 106, 168, 182
  and responsibility, 99–100, 104–5, 159

half empty vs. half full, 3–5, 123–26
  See also emptiness
health, 9
  psychological, 31. *See also* *specific topics*
helplessness, 44
  and health, 9
  learned, 54–55, 57, 58, 61, 91, 178–79
  in animals, 51–55, 57, 61, 91
  See also control
Hofer, Myron, 62–63
hopelessness, 47, 126, 130
hypothalamus, 64

illusion, 5, 10, 59, 176–77
  of an island, 1–3, 10, 192, 195–96. *See also* security
  ability to construct and